inductive nihilism

Damian Melamedoff

Table of Contents

CHAPTER 1: DEFENDING INVARIANTISM

1.0 Introduction:

Within the debate about context-sensitivity, Invariantism is an extreme view. It holds that most words have the same meaning in all contexts, as do most sentences. The goal of this chapter is both exposition and argumentation. First, I want to draw a distinciton between being an invariantist about a particular expression in language on the one hand, and (uppercase 'I') Invariantism as a general semantic theory. Given this distinction, we can use motivations for lower-case 'i' invariantism about some terms to construct the general semantic theory that is Invariantism. In explaining and motivating this general theory, I will also look at some objections to the theory and respond to them.[1]

1.1 Semantic Content:

Over the course of this thesis, I will be assuming a particular orthodox view about to the relationship between a word and its meaning.[2] As the standard story goes, some words have *semantic content*; the semantic content of a word is, very roughly, what the word means.[3] Some sentences have semantic contents, which are (at least partially) determined by the semantic contents of the words in those sentences.[4] The semantic content of a well-formed sentence at a context of utterance of that

---

[1] See Bach (1997; 2008; 2012), Braun (2012; 2013), and especialy Cappelen and Lepore (2005).

[2] For more detailed discussion of the claims that follow, see King (2007) and Soames et al (2014).

[3] Defining "semantic content" is very difficult. Aside from describing the semantic content of a word as its "meaning," one can see semantic content as what the word is about, as what the word "says," or as what is understood when someone understands the word. Another way to understand semantic content is in terms of propositions. The semantic content of an expression in a sentence is what that expression "contributes" to the proposition expressed by the sentence. I am not sure that any of these descriptions is especially clear, but I hope it will be clear enough for my purposes. For more discussion, see Soames (forthcoming)

[4] "Determination" talk here is kept intentionally unclear, since there is disagreement in the literature on propositions about what the relation is between the semantic contents of words and sentences. Frege (1892a, 1892b) and Russell (1903) held that propositions are structured entities that have the semantic contents of words as *constituents*, where the *constentuent of* relation is understood in a way in which the semantic contents of words are somehow "in" the proposition. There is disagreement among neo-Russellians and neo-Fregeans over whether the *constituent of* relation should be taken as primitive or whether it should be reduced to a familiar relation, such as *parthood* or *set membership*. See Soames, et al (forthcoming) Keller, (forthcoming) for discussion of these issues.

Robert Stalnaker (1984) and David Lewis (1986) agreed that the semantic contents of words determine the proposition expressed, but he considered propositions to be sets of truth-supporting circumstances. As a result, the only constituents of a proposition are possible worlds, and not the semantic contents of words.

George Bealer (1993) has argued that propositions are unstructured abstract objects, and therefore do not have any constituents.

sentence is a proposition. So, the sentence "Graham Priest is tall," when uttered at a particular context, expresses a proposition that is at least partially determined by the semantic contents of "Graham Priest" and "is tall." Furthermore, that-clauses are singular expressions that denote propositions. As a result, the clause "that Graham Priest is tall" denotes the proposition expressed by the sentence "Graham Priest is tall."[5] This story admits of certain variations. With regard to words, it leaves open whether the semantic content of "Graham Priest" is the individual Graham Priest, or some "mode of presentation" of the individual Graham Priest, or some set of inference rules about how to use "Graham Priest" in conversation, etc. It also leaves open whether the semantic content of "is tall" is a property/relation, or a mode of presentation of such a property/relation, or a set of rules regarding the use of "is tall" in conversation, etc.[6] With regard to sentences, it leaves open whether the semantic content of a sentence (a proposition) is an abstract Platonic object, a mental event type, or a material composite of its constituents, etc.[7]

The story continues: declarative sentences can have one of two truth values, *true* and *false*.[8] The truth value of a sentence depends on the truth value of the proposition that the sentence expresses.[9] The truth value of the proposition a sentence expresses depends on whether the proposition manages to relate to reality in the right way. Basically, a proposition is true iff what the proposition "says" about reality is how reality is. So, "Graham Priest is tall" would be true just in case the proposition expressed

---

Due to the widespread disagreement over the nature of propositions, I rest content with the modest claim that the semantic content of sentences is *determined* by the semantic content of words without further specifying what the *determination* relation amounts to.

[5]For the *locus classicus* of the view that that-clauses are singular expressions that denote propositions, see Frege (1892a). For some dissenting opinions, see Davidson (1968) , Moltmann (2003).

[6] Millians hold that the semantic contents of words are worldy objects and properties, Fregeans hold that the semantic contents of words are modes of presentation. Inferentialists hold that the semantic contents of words are inference rules. There are many other views in the landscape, but I only mention these three because I take them to be the leading contemporary accounts. For more discussion of Millianism, see Salmon (1986), Braun (2006) and Soames (2002). For more on Fregeanism, see Frege (1892a, 1892b) and Evans (1982). For more on inferentialism, see Brandom (1994).

[7]For a defence of the view that propositions are Platonic Abstracta, see Bealer (1993). For the view that propositions are mental event types, see Soames, et al (2014). For the view that propositions are composed of their constituents, see Caplan and Tillman (ms).

[8] Unlike the rest of the claims made in this story, the claim that all declarative sentences are either true or false will come into question in Chapter 2.

[9]King (2007) denies that the truth-value of a sentence *depends* on the truth-value of the proposition expressed. Regardless, King accepts the weaker claim that a sentence S is true iff the proposition *that S* is true.

by that sentence manages to capture the way reality in fact is. I remain neutral about whether this relation is best thought of as "correspondence with some facts" or in some other way.[10]

Given this basic story about sentences and their truth values, some interesting questions arise. One interesting question is how sentences, semantic contents, and contexts of utterance relate to each other. In "Demonstratives" (1989), David Kaplan introduced the term "character" to discuss precisely this issue. Kaplan defined the character of a term as a function that takes a context as input and outputs the semantic content of that term at that context.[11] So, if we're interested in what the semantic content of "is tall" is at a particular context *C*, we input *C* to the character function of "is tall" and the output will be the semantic content of "is tall". Kaplan also thought that there were two types of character functions. Some terms have a "fixed character". For these terms, the context we input is irrelevant: the semantic content of the term will always be the same. Other terms, however, have a non-fixed character. These terms will have different contents in different contexts. Kaplan's goal in "Demonstratives" was to provide a good account of terms that have non-fixed characters. He listed a few: "yesterday", "I", "here", "that", etc. He did not list terms like "tall", "ready", or "red".

1.2 Contextualism and Invariantism:

Although Kaplan did not list "tall" as a term with non-fixed character, there are some reasons to think that "tall" in fact does have a non-fixed character. Consider, for example, the following story:

> Graham Priest, 6'3", is at a philosophy conference in Oxford. He is the tallest philosopher at the conference. An observer, John, utters the sentence
>
> (A1) John: "Graham Priest is tall".

---

[10]Russell (1903) thinks that propositions are just states of affairs. If so, propositions don't *say* anything about reality, they just *are* reality. As such, Russell accepted an *identity* theory of truth: A proposition is true iff it is identical to some state of affairs. Speaks (Soames, et al. 2014) claims that propositions are properties, and as such they do not represent the world at all. If so, then Speaks has an *instantiation* theory of truth. A proposition is true just in case it is instantiated. Whether the classical conception of propositions or one of these alternative versions is true should not weigh heavily on any of the discussions of this thesis.

[11]Braun (1995) claims that the character should not be understood in terms of a function from possible contexts to contents. Rather, it should be understood hyperintensionally. Although I think that Braun is correct, nothing I say in this thesis hinges on whether we understand character intensionally or hyperintensionally.

Later, due to his passion for basketball, Graham Priest travels to Oklahoma City to meet the Oklahoma City Thunder. The team has very few players under the height of 6'3". As Graham Priest is shaking hands with Kevin Durant (6'10"), an observer, Jane, utters the sentence

(A2) Jane: "Graham Priest is tall".

From these stories, it appears that John is right, but Jane is not. It appears that in the first context, one can truthfully say "Graham Priest is tall", while in the second context, one cannot truthfully say "Graham Priest is tall". Assuming that no proposition can be both true and false, we should conclude that the two utterances of "Graham Priest is tall" failed to express the same proposition.[12] Given Kaplan's terminology above, we would then say that "Graham Priest is tall" has a non-fixed character: it has different contents in different contexts.

With this basic story in hand, there appear to be four ways to explain what is happening in the situations above. One way is to say that the predicate "is tall" has a non-fixed character, which then explains why sentences that include the predicate have non-fixed characters as well.[13] A second way to explain the situations is to say that the predicate "is tall" does have a fixed character, but that the sentence "Graham Priest is tall" is syntactically incomplete: although it is not explicit in the sentence, what the sentence actually says is "Graham Priest is tall relative to *this* comparison group". Since the word "this" has a non-fixed character, we have an explanation for why the sentence has a non-fixed character as well while keeping the character of "is tall" fixed.[14] A third option that we have available is to say that the character of "Graham Priest is tall" is not fixed even though all the terms in the sentence have a fixed character. Maybe because the sentence, although it is syntactically complete, has an unarticulated constituent; a component of

[12]Ironically enough, Graham Priest denies that no proposition can be both true and false. See Priest (2006)
[13]DeRose(2009) has this view when it comes to the verb 'to know'. Lewis (1986) also accepts this view when it comes to the words "possibly" and "necessarily".
[14]This is the option offered by Stanley (2000) and Cappelen and Hawthorne (2009).

the proposition that not expressed by any of the terms (overt or hidden) in the sentence.[15] All of these options are in logical space as an account of how "Graham Priest is tall" has a non-fixed character. Call these explanations "contextualism" about "Graham Priest is tall."

A fourth reaction one could have, the reaction I intend to argue for, is to think that the sentence "Graham Priest is tall" in fact has a fixed character. If one says that, one would think that the sentences uttered by Jane and John express the very same proposition. Call this view "invariantism" about "Graham Priest is tall". The invariantist, unlike the contextualist, has to explain why it is that we think that John and Jane said two different things. Furthermore, the invariantist needs to explain why we are wrong: what reasons do we have to believe that "Graham Priest is tall" has a fixed character?

Invariantists have a few options when dealing with the truth value of "Graham Priest is tall". A Relativist would claim that the proposition expressed (in all contexts) by "Graham Priest is tall" is only true relative to a context. The Relativist would then give up on a non-relative property of truth. The second route an invariantist could take is to be a Radicalist: to reject that the content of "Graham Priest is tall" has a truth value at all, and say that the sentence is incomplete in a way that prevents it from being true or false. A third option would be to be a Monadic Truth Propositionalist: to accept that "Graham Priest is tall" has a unique truth value in all contexts, and explain why the sentence is always true (or always false).[16] These options will be discussed at length in Chapter 2. The goal of the next section, however, is to lay out some motivations for thinking that some version of invariantism about "Graham Priest is tall" is true.

---

[15]Perry (1998) has this view

[16]A view that I am not mentioning here is Subject-Sensitive Invariantism (SSI), as defended by Hawthorne (2004). According to SSI, the truth value of "Graham Priest is tall" changes because (although the proposition is the same) Graham Priest stops being tall when he is around taller people, and becomes tall when he is around shorter people..The reason that I am ignoring this view is that it is not fully general. If two people, having different conversations, utter "Graham Priest is tall" *at the same time*, then the SSI solution no longer works. Suppose that Jane was watching an old recording of Graham Priest with the OKC Thunder, and that she had been doing so *while* John was at a conference with Priest in Oxford. We would still want to say that one sentence was true while the other was false, but SSI doesn't give us an explanation of why. As a result, a fully general solution to these kinds of problems is going to have to appeal to one of the other views anyway.

1.3 Motivation for Invariantism:

There are two ways to argue for invariantism about "Graham Priest is tall." First, one could go one by one through every version of contextualism and provide objections that are specific to those versions. To a large extent, this is what Cappelen and Lepore (2002, 2005) have done. For reasons of space, I won't go into the details of the particular objections against the different versions of contextualism. A second way to argue for Invariantism is to come up with some facts that only an invariantist could account for. This is what I will do in this section.

Consider the sentence:

(A3) "Both John and Jane said that Graham Priest is tall".[17]

The sentence (A3) is true. If (A3) is true, however, then Invariantism must be true. This is because if (A3) is true, then the that-clause in (A3) denotes a proposition that both John and Jane said. But if invariantism is false, then there is no proposition that both John and Jane said. This is because, according to any stripe of contextualism, John and Jane expressed two different propositions when they uttered "Graham Priest is tall".[18] The only way to account for the truth of (A3) is if John and Jane expressed the very same proposition with their utterance of "Graham Priest is tall". But invariantism about "Graham Priest is tall" appears to be the only way to explain such a fact. So, we should think that invariantism is true.

Although this argument is initially quite compelling, it has encountered some resistance. The resistance against this argument has taken two forms. The first form has been to say that Contextualists *can* in fact accomodate for the truth of (A3). The second form of resistance has been to say that (A3) is false, but that this is not a problem because determining semantic content by means of "says-that"

---

[17] This type of argument is due to Cappelen and Lepore (2003, 2005).

[18] McFarlane (2009) defends a view he calls Non-Indexical Contextualism. The view, as applied to our particular sentence, would claim that "Graham Priest is tall" has a fixed character, but has its truth value only relative to a context. As a result, what is "contextual" about McFarlane's view is not the content of a sentence, but its truth conditions. McFarlane's position is perfectly consistent with the truth of (A3), so this might be taken to show that the inference from (A3) to invariantism is invalid. The reader should note, however, that as I've defined Contextualism and Invariantism, Non-Indexical Contextualism is an Invariantist view. As such, it poses no problem for the inference from (A3) to Invariantism.

reports like (A3) gives us unpalatable results anyway. As a consequence, the thought goes, we should think that "says-that" reports are unreliable and provide little or no evidence for what the semantic content of the sentences uttered is. Both of these worries are expressed in Cappelen and Hawthorne (2009), and I will address both of these worries, beginning with the latter.

Cappelen and Hawthorne think that "says-that" reports give us unpalatable results when we apply them to some sentences where it is obvious that their character is non-fixed. They explain:

> To show what's wrong with this and related appeals to [(A3)], we shall again look at the cases of 'left' and 'nearby', which, unlike some of the disputed constructions, have little attendant philosophical emotion and theoretical noise. Interestingly, 'left' and 'nearby' submit to collection patterns of the sort that interests us here:
>
> 24. A: Naomi went to a nearby beach.
> 25. B: Naomi went to a nearby beach.
> 26. C: A and B said that Naomi went to a nearby beach.
> 27. A: Naomi turned left.
> 28. B: Naomi turned left.
> 29. C: A and B said that Naomi turned left.
>
> As we have noted already, [invariantist readings of 26 and 29] in these cases seem problematic. Thus, if these data constitute powerful evidence for semantic uniformity, we will be driven in a more relativistic direction. (Cappelen and Hawthorne, 2009)

The basic argument presented by Cappelen and Hawthorne is as follows:

(B1) 24-25 and 27-28 don't have a fixed character.

(B2) 26 and 29 appear to be accurate reports of 24-25 and 27-28 respectively.

(B3) If (B1) and (B2), then "says-that" reports are unreliable as tests for fixedness of character.

(B4) So, "says-that" reports are unreliable as tests for fixedness of character.

The argument is valid, and (B4) would undermine the motivation for thinking that (A3) is true in the first place. The motivation for (B1) is mostly an intuitive one. It would appear that the direction towards which the word "left" points will depend on which way one is facing. As a result, the content of the word "left" will vary from context to context. It would also appear that the content of "nearby" will depend on where one is. What is *nearby* in Winnipeg is not the same as what is *nearby* in Moscow. The justification for (B2) is the same justification as the one for (A3). (B3) can be justified as follows: 24-25 and 27-28 don't have a fixed character, yet appear to be easily reportable. This should make us doubt the reliability of our reports in the first place.

My main concern with this type of argument stems from (B1). It is not clear to me why saying that the above sentences have a fixed character is so "problematic". More precisely, I don't see why saying that reports 26 and 29 are any *more* problematic than report (A3). Both of them take terms that we would want to give a contextualist treatment, and show that the contextualist treatment will not work.[19] |Cappelen and Hawthorne's arguments here, by themselves, can show one of two things. If 26 and 29 are false, then we have reason to think that sentences containing "left" and "nearby" have non-fixed characters. This is perfectly consistent with invariantism about "Graham Priest is tall", since (A3), unlike 26 and 29, is true. If, on the other hand, 26 and 29 are true, then this tells us that sentences containing "left" and "nearby" have surprisingly fixed characters. The only way in which Cappelen and Hawthorne's argument can provide a motivation for contextualism about "Graham Priest is tall" is if the contextualist had an explanation of the truth of 26 and 29 that could generalize to an explanation about the truth of (A3). I address Cappelen and Hawthorne's proposed explanation below.

Cappelen and Hawthorne's version of contextualism is one in which the sentence "Graham Priest is tall" at some context C expresses the same proposition as the sentence "Graham Priest is tall relative

[19]Cappelen and Lepore (2007) think that it is open for the invariantist about tall to claim that 26 and 29 are only true if the pairs of reported sentences were uttered in sufficiently similar contexts. I am unconvinced by the reply, since it seems like there is no need to know anything about the context of 24-29 to agree with the truth of the reports..

to x" where "x" denotes salient features of C.[20] As a consequence of their view, the proposition expressed by (A1) is a different proposition than the proposition expressed by the sentence (A2). However, Cappelen and Hawthorne claim, there is a way to read (A3) such that it attributes the following property to both John and Jane:

(C1) [being an x such that x says that Graham Priest is tall relative to x's context].

If Cappelen and Hawthorne are right that there is such a reading of (A3), then (A3) is compatible (on that reading) with the denial of invariantism about "Graham Priest is tall". After all, if contextualism of the Cappelen and Hawthorne variety is correct, then both John and Jane instantiate (C1). I will now provide some reasons for thinking that there is no such reading, and that even if there were, the solution would not generalize to all cases of apparent context-sensitivity of "Graham Priest is tall".

The first objection to Cappelen and Hawthorne's argument is due to Braun (2013). Braun shows that if there were a reading of (A3) that attributes (C1) to John and Jane, then there would be a reading of (A3) such that the following argument is invalid:

(A3) Both John and Jane said that Graham Priest is tall

(A4) So, there is something that both John and Jane said.

But the argument above is valid on any reading of (A3). As a consequence, there is no reading of (A3) that attributes (C1) to John and Jane. Similarly, if there were a reading of (A3) that attributes (C1) to John and Jane, then the following argument would also be invalid:

(A3) Both John and Jane said that Graham Priest is tall.

(A5) So, John said that Graham Priest is tall, and Jane also said that.

But there is no reading of (A3) in which this argument is invalid, so there is no reading of (A3) that attributes (C1) to John and Jane.

---

[20]I am extrapolating here. Cappelen and Hawthorne do not explicitly consider sentences with the predicate "is tall", but I don't think it would be unfair to attribute this view to them given what they say about other apparently context-sensitive predicates. See their (2009), Chapter 2.

Suppose that the contextualist has a reply to this Braun-style argument. It is still not the case that the contextualist has a complete explanation of sentences like (A3). As long as there is a context in which (A3) is true, but Cappelen and Hawthorne's reading is false, this would show that Cappelen and Hawthorne's reading cannot explain all apparent cases of accurate reporting. If this were the case, then the contextualist would be committed to explaining away certain cases of context sensitivity in ways similar to what the invariantist does. Once the contextualist goes down this road, it becomes much more difficult to object to the complete invariantist package. I now intend to show that there are cases where (A3) is true, but Cappelen and Hawthorne's reading is false.

Suppose we learn a few more facts about Jane. Jane is a philosopher, and as such, she believes some pretty crazy things. Unlike what most people (and most philosophers) are inclined to think, Jane believes that there is no such relation as the BEING-TALL-RELATIVE-TO relation, but she does believe that there is a *monadic* property of BEING-TALL. Furthermore, Jane is always around people who share her beliefs, and know that they all have these beliefs. When Jane looks at Graham Priest and utters "Graham Priest is tall", it is implausible to think that she instantiates the property (C1). In spite of this, the report in (A3) appears to still be accurate. Even with this new information about the crazy things Jane believes, it is still quite plausible to think that both John and Jane said that Graham Priest is tall. Given this fact, Cappelen and Hawthorne's reading of (A3) is unable to explain all cases in which collective "says-that" reports are true.[21]

Given the present objections, I conclude that Cappelen and Hawthorne's attempt to save contextualism about "Graham Priest is tall" fails. As a result, I believe we not only have good motivation for thinking that the sentence has a fixed character, we also have no good reasons to reject the reliability of "says-that" reports for determining fixed-ness of character.

[21]We might worry that the content of Jane's utterance should have nothing to do with Jane's intentions or the conversational record. But this would be to give up on one of the main motivations for contextualism about "Graham Priest is tall."

1.4 Defining Invariantism:

Given my previous discussion about "Graham Priest is tall", we might ask ourselves whether there is any systematic way to determine whether a particular sentence has a fixed character. I believe that the answer is yes, and that "says-that" reports are the key to such a theory. Consider the following stories:

(D1) Joe Biden, sitting in front of Barack Obama in the White House, utters the sentence "Barack Obama is here".

(D2) Vladimir Putin, sitting in his office in Moscow, utters the sentence "Barack Obama is here".

Similar to our motivations for contextualism about "Graham Priest is tall", we might say something in favour of contextualism about "Barack Obama is here". The sentence expresses different propositions in the two different contexts, and has different truth conditions. There are different accounts we could give about how this happens. First, we could say that the word "here" has a non-fixed character. Second, we could say that the sentence "Barack Obama is here" has a hidden term in it which accounts for the non-fixed charater of the sentence. Finally, we could say that the sentence has a non-fixed character even though none of the terms in the sentence have non-fixed characters.

Just like one could be a contextualist about "Barack Obama is here", one could be an invariantist about "Barack Obama is here". As far as I'm aware, nobody has tried this, but it is at the very least a position in logical space to be an invariantist about this sentence. As a result, we can ask whether the argument for invariantism about "Graham Priest is tall" translates into an argument for invariantism about "Barack Obama is here". The question, then, is whether:

(D3) "Both Biden and Putin said that Barack Obama is here"

is true. But, when we look at (D3), we can see that the sentence is not true. If Biden utters (D3), he would be saying something false, since Putin did not say that Obama is in DC. If Putin utters (D3), he would be saying something false, since Biden did not say that Obama is in Moscow. And if I, in

Winnipeg, uttered (D3), I would be saying something false, since neither Biden nor Putin said that Obama is in Winnipeg. We should think, then, that (D3) is false. But if we do, then we don't have a compelling argument for invariantism about "Barack Obama is here".[22]

Given these considerations, we can now have a principled way to define a general semantic view: Invariantism (with an uppercase 'I'). Invariantism is the view that states that sentences that would be *accurately* reported, were they to be reported by reports like (A3) and (D3), have a fixed character.[23] We can then provide a definition of the Basic Set of Context Sensitive Terms (AKA "Basic Set"), as follows:

Basic Set: {x: x is not in any sentences that have a fixed character}

We can see that words like "this", "I" and "here" will belong to the Basic Set, since any sentence in which they appear will have a non-fixed character.[24] We can also see that words like "tall" and "ready" will appear in some sentences with fixed characters. As a consequence of this, we can give an account of words with non-fixed characters in terms of sentences with non-fixed characters. We can now have a full definition of invariantism about both terms and sentences:

Invariantism:

- A *sentence* has a fixed character just in case it can be accurately reported by "says-that" reports.

- A *word* has a fixed character just in case it appears in some sentence which has a fixed character.

1.5 Conclusion:

[22]There are some cases where it would appear correct for Putin to say "that's what I said!" after Biden says "Obama is here." I am worried, however, that this may just be a case of speaking loosely, and that Putin would recant his statement if Biden (still in DC) asked him "you said that Obama is here?" I don't think this is the case with words like "tall".

[23] I am assuming that counterfactuals with impossible antecedents are not all vacuously true, but rather have substantive truth values. For a dissenting opinion, see Lewis (1986).

[24]One thing we might worry about is that there might be languages where some terms appear only in sentences where a member of the Basic Set appears, yet that term is not context sensitive. For example, we might have a term *t* that means the same thing as the word 'tall', but as a syntactic rule only appears in sentences in which the word 'here' is used. This term would have a fixed character but qualify as a member of the Basic Set under my definition. As far as I'm aware, English does not have some terms, so I'm happy to use the definition above. Given these possible counterexamples, however, I am reluctant to put that much weight into it as an analysis of the Basic Set.

In this chapter, I have argued that sentences like "Graham Priest is tall" have fixed characters. I have shown that contextualist responses to collective "says-that" reports fail. I have also given a complete definition of Invariantism as a systematic semantic theory, which takes "says-that" reports as its starting point.

But there are still some questions that the Invariantist needs to answer. The first question to be asked is what the content of "Graham Priest is tall" is. Second, we can ask what the content of the *terms* in the sentence "Graham Priest is tall" is. In the next two chapters I intend to defend a collection of theses that answer this question. The theses Are:

Monadic Truth Propositionalism: the contents of sentences like "Graham Priest is tall" are propositions, which have non-relative truth values.

Nihilism: the predicate "is tall" does not denote anything at all.

Russellian-Compatibilism: the conjunction of Propositionalism and Nihilism is consistent with neo-Russellian accounts of propositions.

Neo-Russellianism is the conjunction of the following views:

(I) The semantic content of a name, if any, is the object it refers to, if any.

(II) The semantic content of a predicate, if any, is the property or relation that it expresses, if any.

(III) The semantic content of a sentence, if any, is a structured proposition.

(IV) The semantic contents of names and predicates in a sentence are the constituents of the proposition expressed by that sentence.

(V) Some expressions have semantic content.

I defend Monadic Truth Propositionalism and Nihilism because I think that they are true. I defend Russellian-Compatibilism for a different reason. Although I believe that neo-Russellianism about propositions is true, my main motivation for this defence is different. I believe that there is some apparent tensions between neo-Russellianism and my other two views; tensions that do not appear with non-Russellian accounts of propositions. Furthermore, since neo-Russellianism is among the leading theories of propositions, it would be an unfortunate consequence of my position if it ruled out one of the main competitors in that area. As a result, my position would be better if it were compatible with neo-Russellianism. Chapter 2 is intended to be an argument for both Propositionalism and Nihilism. Chapter 3 is intended as a defence of Russellian-Compatibilism, as well as a defence of Nihilism from various other objections.

CHAPTER 2: HOW NOT TO BE AN INVARIANTIST

2.0 Introduction

Invariantism can be divided into four different versions. The goal of this chapter is to show that three of these versions are false. The four versions of Invariantism are Restricted Property Invariantism, Minimalism, Radicalism, and Nihilism. I will defend my preferred view, Nihilism, in Chapter 3. In this chapter I will explain and argue against the first three versions of Invariantism. If my arguments in Chapter 1 are sound, then we should think that Invariantism is true. If my arguments in this chapter are sound, then we should think that Nihilism is the only viable version of Invariantism. We can then, via *modus ponens*, conclude that Nihilism is true. For the sake of simplicity, my discussion here will be restricted to one-place predicates. I believe that everything I have to say can be translated without much effort both into talk of context-sensitive relational predicates, and talk of context-sensitive operators.[25]

Restricted Property Invariantism and Minimalism both claim that context sensitive one-place predicates denote monadic properties. Where they disagree is with regards to which property these predicates denote. A Minimalist will claim that the property denoted by some predicate 'is F' is one that is intensionally equivalent to the property of BEING-F-IN-SOME-WAY-OR-OTHER (see Cappelen and Lepore, 2005; Braun (2012)).[26] The Restricted Property Invariantist will reject this claim.

An example might illustrate the distinction between these two views. According to both Restricted Property and Minimalism, the statement 'Graham Priest is tall' attributes to Priest the one-place property of BEING-TALL. We still have, however, the metaphysical question of what it takes for

[25] There is a question here about whether singular terms such as proper names can be context sensitive, or just ambiguous. I will remain non-committal about this fact.

[26] Cappelen and Lepore are very non-committal on what the property of *being tall* is supposed to be. At some points, the appear to endorse a version of Restricted Property Invariantism, but some of their arguments by analogy to *being red* would appear to commit them to what I'm calling Minimalism. Braun is much more explicit, when he states that the term 'possibly' denotes "*being possible*," where this is "a very weak sort of possibility. Any proposition that is metaphysically possible, nomologically possible, or epistemically possible for any agent, is possible in this sense." Although "possibly" is not a first-order predicate, everything I have to say here should apply to the term as well.

somebody (in this case Priest) to instantiate the property of BEING-TALL. A Minimalist would say that all it takes for somebody to instantiate BEING-TALL is that they be tall in some way or other. We can call this account of BEING-TALL the "minimal property" of BEING-TALL.

A Restricted Property Invariantist will not accept this account of the property of BEING-TALL. They may object, for example, that this property includes too many things, including things that just are not tall. An ant may be taller than a bacterium, but that does not mean an ant is tall. As a consequence, a Restricted Property Invariantist will say that the property of BEING-TALL which the predicate 'is tall' denotes is more restricted (applies to fewer objects) than the minimal property of BEING-TALL.

Radicalists reject the claim that context-sensitive predicates denote a property of the same adicity as the predicate. According to Radicalism, the predicate 'is tall' does not denote any monadic property. Instead, 'is tall' denotes something else. The predicate 'is tall' may denote, for example, a relation (the relation of BEING-TALLER-THAN, or BEING-TALL-IN-COMPARISON-TO). Since the second relatum will be different in different contexts (but the semantic content of the sentence will not), then the second relatum will not be included in the semantic content of the sentence. A consequence of this is that the sentence"'Graham Priest is tall" fails to encode a complete proposition. As a result, proponents of Radicalism think that sentences containing terms like "tall" encode *propositional radicals*. A propositional radical is an entity that has the structure of a proposition but is missing some key component that would allow us to evaluate it for truth or falsity. Propositional radicals are therefore not truth-apt, and neither is the sentence 'Graham Priest is tall'.[27]

Finally, Nihilism agrees with Radicalism that context sensitive one-place predicates fail to denote monadic properties, but rejects that such predicates denote something else. Instead, context sensitive terms are treated as non-denoting predicates. Since sentences containing non-denoting terms can still be truth-apt, it does not follow from Nihilism that sentences containing context sensitive terms

[27] The main chamption of Radicalism is Bach (1997, 2008). Soames also sometimes endorses something like Radicalism (2005, forthcoming). Recanati (2004) claims that if he were to accept that there is purely semantic content, then it would be a propositional radical.

fail to encode propositions.[28] In my particular flavor of Nihilism, having a context sensitive term is no obstacle at all to a sentence's ability to encode a proposition and be evaluated for truth. I will not discuss the virtues and vices of Nihilism any further in this chapter; I will reserve this task to Chapter 3.

2.1 Restricted Property Invariantism:

Among the four views presented above, Restricted Property Invariantism seems to have the most intuitive plausibility. In the general literature, however, it is very hard to find an Invariantist who endorses a version of this view. Cappelen and Lepore (2006) start out non-committal between Restricted Property Invariantism and Minimal Property Invariantism, by claiming that figuring out which properties are denoted by context-sensitive terms should be the job of metaphysicians, not philosophers of language.[29] By the end of their book, however, they tentatively endorse Minimal Property Invariantism.[30] Given that Restricted Property Invariantism sounds so plausible in comparison to other versions of Invariantism, it would seem curious that no versions of it have been defended. I think the reason why Restricted Property Invariantism has not been defended is that every version of it is indefensible. The reason is that there is, in principle, no way to determine which version of Restricted Property Invariantism is the right one.

I take it that Cappelen and Lepore are right when they claim that it is metaphysicians (and not philosophers of language) who should be concerned with questions about what it takes to instantiate some property. It would be pertinent, then, to inquire into how it is that metaphysicians figure out what it takes to instantiate some property. It seems to me that the standard strategy is to look at cases in

---

[28] Some reject this claim. This includes Meinongians, who believe that there are no non-denoting terms (see Priest, 2005), as well as some Russellians, who believe that sentences with non-denoting terms encode gappy propositions, which lack truth values (Salmon 1998; Adams et al., 2002).

[29] "We're most certainly *not* claiming that something is red just in case it is *red in some way* (or *in some respect* or *under some conditions*). Our view is that to be red *is* just to be red. We're adamant about this short answer for two reasons. First, we refuse to mix metaphysics and semantics..." (2005, p.158)

[30] "Imagine someone registering this objection: Doesnt' that make it very easy, indeed, too easy, to be red? Doesn't it render both the White House and Uma Thurman's eyes red? Both things, after all, are red *on some surface under some conditions*? Reply: Maybe, yes. When you think hard about what it is to be red, maybe that's all it takes. If so, then it turns out that it's not that hard to be red." (2005, p.160)

which we might claim that some object *o* instantiates some property *F*, and ask whether or not we would in fact make that claim. If we would, then we conclude that *o* has what it takes to instantiate *F*. If we do this with a sufficient amount of objects, we can now compare all the objects that have what it takes to instantiate *F* and infer what it is that they all have in common, in virtue of which they instantiate *F*.

The problem with this strategy for context sensitive predicates like "is tall| is that there is always a case, for anything that is tall in some way or other, where we would assent to the claim that it is tall. We can illustrate this point by looking back at the ant example that was given in the original formulation of Restricted Property Invariantism. Suppose we want to decide whether ants have the monadic property of BEING-TALL. In order to decide whether ants have or lack this property, we would look at cases where we might be inclined to assert that ants are tall, and see if we would in fact make such an assertion. But there are some contexts where we would say that ants are tall, and there are some contexts in which we would not say that ants are tall. Since, by the assumptions of Invariantism, the property denoted by "is tall" (if any) is the same across all contexts, there is no principled way to decide whether an ant has or lacks the property of BEING-TALL.[31] The resulting problem is that we can have two Restricted Property theories of the following kind:

(a) Objects have the property of being tall iff they are at least 5 cm in height.

(b) Objects have the property of being tall iff they are at least 10 cm in height.

Restricted Property Invariantists have no way of arguing for one of (a) and (b) over the other. As a result, it becomes impossible to support a particular version of Restricted Property Invariantism as opposed to another. This does not mean that Restricted Property Invariantism is false, only that it is an untenable position. The position is untenable due to the fact that we cannot choose which of the candidate properties is the property of BEING-TALL. Our inability to choose, however, does not mean that it is not the case that one of the candidate properties *is* the property of BEING-TALL. The arguments,

[31] A version of this objection attributed to Hawthorne by Cappelen and Lepore (2006).

so far, at best give us some sort of scepticism about BEING-TALL.[32, 33]

The untenability of the view might be enough for some to reject it, but I think that more can be done to argue against it. This is because Restricted Property Invariantism is untenable in an interesting way. Specifically, Restricted Property Invariantism is untenable in a way which allows us to construct an argument for why any version of it is false. The basic idea is as follows. Suppose (a) is the correct theory of which property the predicate 'is tall' refers to. Presumably, the reason why 'is tall' refers to a property that has (a) conditions rather than (b) conditions is that the property that has (a) conditions is more natural, more fundamental, more joint-carving.[34] But there seem to be no reasons to think that a property that meets the (a) conditions is any more natural than a property that meets the (b) conditions. The argument generalizes, and we can formalize it as follows:

> (A1) If Restricted Property Invariantism is true, then some particular version of Restricted Property Invariantism, A, is true.
>
> (A2) If A is true, then the instantiation conditions for properties expressed by context-sensitive predicates which A specifies are more natural than those of other versions of Restricted Property Invariantism.
>
> (A3) It is not the case that the instantiation conditions for properties expressed by context-sensitive predicates which A specifies are more natural than those of other versions of

[32] We might consider a Restricted Property Invariantist who adopts an epistemicist position towards tallness, similar to the kind of epistemicism about vague predicates proposed by Williamson (1994). There are, however, major differences between these two versions of epistemicism. In the case of the vagueness of "tall", there are some cases where we are certain that an object is tall. In fact, the taller an object gets, the more certain we are. But in the case of context sensitivity, this is not the case. This is because, unlike in the case of vagueness, *every* candidate property is equally likely to be the one picked out by "tall". This makes an epistemicist position much harder to hold in the case of context-sensitivity than it is in the case of vagueness.

Regardless, even if the difficulty in finding the property of tallness can be attributed to vagueness, this is not so with other examples of allegedly context-sensitive predicates, such as 'is ready' and 'is strong enough'. So, even if one could be a Restricted Property Invariantist about "is tall", it still would not give us a solution to other cases of context sensitivity.

[33] A worry one might have is that, in the particular case of "tall," there are some better candidates: Presumably the tallest person is a better candidate for being tall than the second tallest person. This thought results from restricting our account of tallness only to intrinsic height. But there are other tallness relational properties that we might be interested in as well. Consider for example the property of BEING-TALL-WHEN-MEASURED FROM-KNEE-TO-HIP. It is quite possible for the intrinsically tallest beings to not have the above property in some contexts. As a result, we should still be inclined to say that no candidate property is the best suited to be the property of BEING-TALL. Also, as in the previous note, vagueness won't solve problems with predicates such as 'is ready' and 'is strong enough'.

[34] See Sider (2011) and Lewis (1983) for a more detailed discussion of naturalness.

Restricted Property Invariantism.

(A4) So, Restricted Property Invariantism is false.

(A1) is a fairly trivial point. (A2) is a precise formulation of what it would take for a particular version of Restricted Property Invariantism to be true. What is required is that the predicates that we usually use refer to some property that is more natural than the properties to which other versions of Restricted Property Invariantism would want our predicates to refer. (A3) is what I take to be the now obvious claim that no such version of Restricted Property Invariantism can accomplish this. The example used above with the property of BEING-TALL is one that could be constructed for any context sensitive predicate. (A4) follows from the first three premises. As a consequence, we should not only think that Restricted Property Invariantism is untenable, we should think that every version of it is false.

2.2 Minimalism:

Minimalism avoids the objection above. When wondering whether an object meets the conditions for instantiating a property denoted by a context-sensitive predicate, a Minimal Property Invariantist will claim that the object meets the conditions just in case it has the relevant property in some way or another. For example, in wondering whether an ant is tall, we ask ourselves if there is any situation in which we would say that an ant is tall. If the answer is 'yes', then the ant has the monadic property of BEING-TALL. The thought is that this criterion gives us a principled way of accepting Minimalism where no version of Restricted Property Invariantism does. A predicate of the form 'is *F*' denotes a property that is intensionally equivalent to the property BEING-F-IN-SOME-WAY-OR-OTHER.

The main objection against Minimalism has a significant history. It has had sufficient impact on Invariantist views that Cappelen and Lepore (2005) gave it a name ("the Metaphysical Objection") and dedicated an entire chapter of *Insensitive Semantics* to trying to refute it. Consider, for example, Bach's (2006) objection to Cappelen and Lepore's Invariantism:

But what if metaphysical consultation revealed that 'being ready' and 'having had

> enough' do not express properties but, rather, property functions or something of the sort? Then Cappelen and Lepore would have to conclude that sentences like 'Art is ready' and 'Bart has had enough' do not express propositions after all… The question is whether having had enough is a property, indeed the one that [all people who have had enough of something] share.

Cappelen and Lepore also acknowledge this as a threat to their Minimalist position:

> The Semantic Minimalist says that an utterance of 'A is red' semantically expresses the proposition *that A is red*. He also says that this proposition is not the same proposition as the proposition *that A is red on the inside*, or as *that A is red on the outside*, or as *that A is red when looked at through red sunglasses*, or as *that A is red in normal light*. It's just the proposition *that A is red*. But which proposition is that? What, for example, is it to be just red? What is it that all these things (those that are red when seen through red sunglasses, red on the inside, red in the dark, red on the outside, red when washed, etc.) have in common? What is the state of affairs that the proposition *that A is red* picks out? (2005, p. 157-8)

The objection, using the predicate 'is tall' as an example is as follows:

> (B1) If Minimalism is true, then there is some monadic property of BEING-TALL that the predicate 'is tall' denotes.
>
> (B2) There is no monadic property of BEING-TALL that the predicate 'is tall' denotes.
>
> (B3) So, Minimalism is false.

The first thing one might notice about this argument is that it is very similar to the one given against Restricted Property Invariantism, but generalized. The general justification that is given for (B2) by opponents of Cappelen and Lepore's Invariantism takes the form of a puzzled look. It seems absurd to many philosophers that there could be a monadic property of BEING-TALL in the first place, let alone one which all tall things have. I share this feeling of puzzlement, but puzzled looks are not arguments, so it would be better if there could be a better way to justify (B2). There is, *prima facie*, no reason to think that there couldn't be a monadic property that all tall things have. There is also, *prima facie*, no reason to think that the predicate 'is tall' couldn't denote such a property. At the same time, there doesn't seem to be any reason to think that there is in fact such a property.

Cappelen and Lepore offer motivation for thinking that there is a property of BEING-TALL that all tall things share.

> Some red things are red on the inside, some are red on the outside, some are red when scrubbed, some are red in the dark, some are red when peeled, some are red when seen through red sunglasses, etc. You might ask the age-old metaphysical query: What do they all have in common? What is this property of being red that they all share? (2005, p.160)
>
> What this reveals, we think, is that our opponents, i.e. those who claim that there is no such thing as being red simpliciter, should, in order to be consistent, say that there's a puzzle about the very idea of two or more things sharing properties or engaging in the same activities. (2005, p. 163)

Cappelen and Lepore's argument for the existence of a monadic property of BEING-TALL (which, of course, generalizes to other context-sensitive predicates) seems to be the following:

(C1) If there is no monadic property of BEING-TALL, then there is nothing that all tall things have in common.

(C2) There is something that all tall things have in common.

(C3) So, there is a monadic property of BEING-TALL.

In defence of (C1), Cappelen and Lepore ask us to consider someone who rejects the existence of the monadic property of BEING-TALL, and instead accepts the existence of a relation of BEING-TALL-RELATIVE-TO-COMPARISON-CLASS-*C*. The same questions that we ask of BEING-TALL can be asked of this relational property. What do all things that are tall with respect to C have in common? What about all the things that are tall with respect to C when they are 20 years old? What do they have in common with the things that are tall with respect to C when they are 100 years old? Cappelen and Lepore's thought is that any answer to these questions is one that we can give to the question of what it is to be tall simpliciter. I take premise (C2) to be obviously true.[35]

I believe that Cappelen and Lepore's justification for (C1) misses the point of the objection. The issue is not whether there is a property that all tall things have in common. The issue is whether this property is the property of BEING-TALL. In fact, (C1) is false for exactly that reason. It may be the case that all tall things have the property of BEING-TALL-IN-SOME-WAY-OR-OTHER, so it is not the case that they also need the monadic property of BEING-TALL in order to have something in common. Cappelen and Lepore could claim here that BEING-TALL-IN-SOME-WAY-OR-OTHER just is the monadic property of BEING-TALL. I will argue against this proposal shortly.

There may be other motivations one may have for believing that the predicate "is tall" denotes the monadic property of BEING-TALL. One could think that every predicate refers to a property, and that a one-place predicate will refer to a monadic property. If so, then the predicate "is tall" must denote some monadic property. For reasons stated above, no version of Restricted Property Invariantism will give us the property we want. Since the minimal property of BEING-TALL is the only available property that is left, we should conclude that "is tall" refers to that property. Formalized, the argument is as follows:

(D1) All predicates denote a property.

(D2) If a one place predicate denotes a property, then the property denoted is a monadic property.

(D3) If (D1) and (D2), then "is tall" denotes some monadic property.

(D4) If "is tall" denotes some monadic property, then it denotes the minimal property of BEING-TALL.

(D5) So, "is tall" denotes the minimal property of BEING-TALL.

[35] Debates over the existence of universals are as old as philosophy itself, and this is not the place to engage in them. I unapologetically accept the existence of universals for the remainder of this thesis.

As we will later see, Radicalists will deny (D2). The suspicious premise, I believe, is (D1). There are some paradoxes associated with the thesis that all predicates denote a property. Consider the predicate "is non-self-instantiating". If this predicate denotes a property, it would be the property of BEING-NON-SELF-INSTANTIATING. But if the property of BEING-NON-SELF-INSTANTIATING exists, then we can ask whether it instantiates itself. If it does, then it fails to be non-self instantiating, so it does not instantiate itself. If it doesn't instantiate itself, then it is non-self instantiating, so it does instantiate itself. As a consequence, the property of BEING-NON-SELF-INSTANTIATING cannot exist. But if it does not exist, then the predicate "is non-self-instantiating" does not denote it. It is implausible that the predicate "is non-self-instantiating" manages to denote some other property given how it was defined. As a consequence, we should think that the predicate "is non-self-instantating" fails to denote any property. But now we have an argument against (D1)

(E1) If (D1) is true, then the predicate "is non-self-instantating" denotes a property.

(E2) The predicate "is non-self-instantating" does not denote a property.

(E3) So, (D1) is not true.

There is a further reason to think that not all predicates denote a property. This is because the view that all predicates denote commits one to the claim that all terms denote an object. Suppose otherwise. Then there is some term, *t*, which fails to refer to an object. But we can now construct the predicate "is identical to *t*". If this predicate denotes a property, then the property must be one which includes the referent of *t* as one of its components. But there is no referent of *t*! So there can't be such a property. We now have the argument:

(F1) If (D1) is true, then every term denotes.

(F2) Some terms don't denote.

(F3) So (D1) is false.

The justification for (F1) is above. Anyone short of a Meinongian should accept (F2).[36]

[36] I understand a Meinongian to be someone who claims that there are no non-denoting terms. For more on Meinongianism, see Priest (2005)

There is a third argument that a Minimalist could give to motivate the view that there is a monadic property of BEING-TALL. Consider the sentence "Graham Priest is tall". This sentence is *true*. But if the sentence is true, then Graham Priest instantiates the property of BEING-TALL. So there is a property of BEING-TALL, and it is denoted by "is tall". Formalized, the argument is:

(G1) "Graham Priest is tall" is true.

(G2) If (G1), then Graham Priest instantiates BEING-TALL.

(G3) If Graham Priest instantiates BEING-TALL, then "is tall" denotes the monadic property of BEING-TALL.

(G4) So, "is tall" denotes the monadic property of BEING-TALL.

While this argument appears initially compelling, there are reasons to be sceptical about (G1). In some contexts "Graham Priest is tall" appears to be true; in some contexts "Graham Priest is tall" appears not to be true (if a sentence is not true, then we have no reason to, on the basis of its truth value, suppose that any terms in that sentence denote). It is not clear why we should then take the contexts in which the sentence appears to be true as any more evidence than the contexts in which it appears to be false. But if that's right, we at best have reasons to be sceptical about (G1). But if so, we at best have reasons to be sceptical about the monadic property of BEING-TALL. As a result, this argument does not give us motivation to believe in the existence of BEING-TALL.

The discussion above was intended to undermine the motivation to think that there is in fact a monadic property of BEING-TALL that "is tall" denotes. But none of the arguments above entail that there is no such property. I will now give some reasons for thinking that there is no property of BEING-TALL that "is tall" denotes.

The monadic property of BEING-TALL, if there is such a thing, has the same instantiation conditions as the property of BEING-TALL-IN-SOME-WAY-OR-OTHER. There are three ways in which this could be the case. First, it might be that the monadic property of BEING-TALL just is the property of BEING-TALL-IN-SOME-WAY-OR-OTHER. Second, it could be the case that the monadic property of BEING-

TALL is a property that is metaphysically dependent on the property BEING-TALL-IN-SOME-WAY-OR-OTHER. This is to say that objects instantiate the property of BEING-TALL in virtue of the fact that they instantiate the property of BEING-TALL-IN-SOME-WAY-OR-OTHER. Finally, we could think that the property of BEING-TALL is metaphysically independent (but intensionally equivalent to) the property of BEING-TALL-IN-SOME-WAY-OR-OTHER. This would be to say that necessarily, objects instantiate the property of BEING-TALL when they are tall in some way or another, but not in virtue of their being tall in some way or another. I will first take on the first two options together.

What the first two views agree on is that the property of BEING-TALL is no more fundamental than the property of BEING-TALL-IN-SOME-WAY-OR-OTHER. In the first case, it is because they are equally fundamental (they are the same property); in the second case it is because the property of BEING-TALL-IN-SOME-WAY-OR-OTHER is more fundamental than the property of BEING-TALL. We can now construct an argument against either of these views.

(H1) If the property of BEING-TALL is no more fundamental than the property of BEING-TALL-IN-SOME-WAY-OR-OTHER, then the property of BEING-TALL is no more natural than the property of BEING-TALL-IN-SOME-WAY-OR-OTHER

(H2) If the property of BEING-TALL is no more natural than the property of BEING-TALL-IN-SOME-WAY-OR-OTHER, then if the property of BEING-TALL-IN-SOME-WAY-OR-OTHER is not sufficiently natural to be denoted by "is tall", then the property of BEING-TALL is not sufficiently natural to be denoted by "is tall".

(H3) The property of BEING-TALL-IN-SOME-WAY-OR-OTHER is not sufficiently natural to be denoted by "is tall".

(H4) So, if the property of BEING-TALL is no more fundamental than the property of BEING-TALL-IN-SOME-WAY-OR-OTHER, then the property of BEING-TALL is not sufficiently natural to be denoted by "is tall".

(H5) If (H4), then the first two versions of Minimalism are false.

(H6) So, the first two versions of Minimalism are false.

I will now provide a more thorough defence of each premise.

Premise (H1) is based on what I take to be a basic principle regarding the relation between fundamentality and naturalness. This is the principle that for any two objects *a* and *b*, if *a* is more natural than *b*, then *a* is more fundamental than *b*. I take this principle to be fairly intuitively compelling, and short of any counter-examples, I can't think of a reason to reject it.

Premise (H2) says something that I take to be trivially true. Suppose BEING-TALL is no more natural than BEING-TALL-IN-SOME-WAY-OR-OTHER, and suppose that BEING-TALL-IN-SOME-WAY-OR-OTHER is not sufficiently natural to be denoted by "is tall". What is wrong with BEING-TALL-IN-SOME-WAY-OR-OTHER, by hypothesis, is that it fails to be natural enough to be denoted by "is tall". But, also by hypothesis, BEING-TALL is no more natural than BEING-TALL-IN-SOME-WAY-OR-OTHER. So BEING-TALL would also fail to be natural enough to be denoted by "is tall".

Since (H3) is the most controversial premise, I will omit it for now, and return to it at the end of the defence. (H4) is true by Hypothetical Syllogism. For a defence of (H5), suppose (H4) is true. Then either BEING-TALL is more fundamental than BEING-TALL-IN-SOME-WAY-OR-OTHER, or BEING-TALL is not sufficiently natural to be denoted by "is tall". If the first disjunct is the case, then the first two versions of Minimal Property Invariantism are false. This is because the first two versions of Minimal Property Invariantism claim that BEING-TALL is not more fundamental than BEING-TALL-IN-SOME-WAY-OR-OTHER. If the second disjunct is true, then "is tall" does not denote the monadic property of BEING-TALL, and Minimal Property Invariantism as a whole is false. Either way, on the assumption that (H4) is true, the first two versions of Minimal Property Invariantism are false. (H6) follows by *modus ponens*.

Here is the defence of (H3). The property of BEING-TALL-IN-SOME-WAY-OR-OTHER is a highly disjunctive property. It is built up of several distinct and more fundamental properties such as the property of BEING-TALL-WHEN-WEARING-HIGH-HEELS, BEING-TALL-IN-COMPARISON-TO-AN-ANT,

BEING-TALL-AFTER-TEA-TIME, etc. The fact that we have to use a clause like "in some way or another" to even express the property should be an indication of how non-natural the property itself is. In fact, we should think that specifications of "is tall" given in (a) and (b) of section 2.1 are more natural than BEING-TALL-IN-SOME-WAY-OR-OTHER. But if (a) and (b) are not sufficiently natural to be denoted by "is tall", then neither would be the preoperty of BEING-TALL-IN-SOME-WAY-OR-OTHER. Therefore, BEING-TALL-IN-SOME-WAY-OR-OTHER is not sufficiently natural to be denoted by "is tall".

One way a Minimalist could attempt to avoid these criticisms would be to appeal to use-facts. A Minimalist could try to show that the way we use the predicate "is tall" forces it to refer to the non-natural property of BEING-TALL or of BEING-TALL-IN-SOME-WAY-OR-OTHER. I think this would be a very difficult argument for the Minimalist to make. First of all, use facts for the predicate "is tall" will vary from context to context, and, as I have argued above, the predicate does not have to be used with the intent to refer to the property of BEING-TALL-IN-SOME-WAY-OR-OTHER. Furthermore, normal speakers do not have a sufficiently sophisticated understanding of the semantics of "is tall" to be able to consciously refer to a property as strange as BEING-TALL. Finally, though I don't have conclusive evidence for this, my asking people whether they believe in a monadic property of tallness has yielded almost unanimous agreement, both among philosophers and non-philosophers, that there is no such property. This would make it unlikely that they would use the predicate "is tall" to attempt to denote such a property.

The third option survives these criticisms, but at a significant cost. The third option claims that the property of BEING-TALL is not dependent on the property of BEING-TALL-IN-SOME-WAY-OR-OTHER. This is to say, things are tall when they are tall in some way or another, but they are not tall in virtue of being tall in some way or another. Unfortunately, I don't have a knock-down argument against this position. All I can do here is to give a puzzled look. I think, however, that the puzzled look is more warranted in this situation than before. The reason why a puzzled look was not warranted as a way to dismiss Minimal Property Invariantism is that the Minimal Property Invariantist offered an explanation of what the strange property of BEING-TALL is: a complex property built out of (or identical to) the property of BEING-TALL-IN-SOME-WAY-OR-OTHER. But now the Invariantist has no explanation: the property of BEING-TALL is some fundamental property that all tall things have independently of their being tall in some way or other. This is a puzzling property, and one that we should do without if we can help it. So while this version of Minimal Property Invariantism is not vulnerable to my objections above, this is because the view posits strange properties as explanations and fails to give us an account of what these properties are like. I take this to be a sufficient reason to reject the view.[37]

2.3 Radicalism:

The thought behind Radicalism is that some sentences have all of the syntactical components to compose a grammatically well-formed declarative sentence, but are missing some semantic component that would enable the proposition to be truth-evaluable. The thought may be illustrated as follows:

(S1) "Graham Priest is tall."

(S2) "Graham Priest is tall in comparison to."

(S2) is both syntactically and semantically deficient. Syntactically, it has a relational predicate that is missing an object. Semantically, the relational predicate encodes a relation, but a relatum is missing. According to the proponent of Radicalism, (S1) is not syntactically deficient at all, but it is semantically deficient in the same way as (S2) is. The semantic *content* of (S1) and (S2), according to the Radicalist, is the same.[38] The semantic structure, however, is different: (S1) encodes something with the same structure as a proposition, while (S2) does not. Since the proposition-like entity encoded

[37]We might think that a way out of these objections is to become a Relativist about truth: the predicate "is tall" still denotes the minimal property of BEING-TALL, but this is less strange when we see that the sentence "Graham Priest is tall" is not true *simpliciter*. McFarlane (2009) proposes such an amendment to Cappelen and Lepore. I, however, cannot see why this would get the Relativist out of this problem. The argument isn't an argument for the sentence not being true, it is an argument for there being no property of BEING-TALL. The alleged property does not get any less strange when we change some of the properties of the propositions it is in.

[38] This presupposes that (S2) has any semantic content at all, which a Radicalist may deny. Since the example is mostly illustrative, I don't think this is much of an issue.

by (S1) is semantically incomplete and it is the semantic content of a sentence that determines its truth conditions, (S1) does not have any truth conditions on the Radicalist view. Radicalists like to say that the semantic content of context-sensitive sentences is a propositional radical, or a propositional skeleton, which has many things in common with propositions, but lacks truth conditions, and thus lacks a truth value.[39]

Unfortunately, it is hard to find what the motivation for Radicalism is. Generally, the arguments given for Radicalism take the following form:

(I1) Invariantism is true.

(I2) Minimalism is false.

(I3) If (I1) and (I2), then Radicalism is true.

(I4) So Radicalism is true.

The biggest problem is that Radicalists spend most of their time arguing for (I1) and (I2), and take (I3) for granted. It should be clear by now why I object to this. I argued for (I1) in Chapter 1, and have spent a significant section of this Chapter 2 arguing for (I2). It is (I3) which I am looking to reject, in order to endorse Nihilism. This creates a problem, since I take it that the argument an Invariantist will give for (I3) is as follows:

(J1) Nihilism is false.

(J2) If Nihilism is false, then (I3) is true.

(J3) So (I3) is true.

I think (J2) is true. I can't think of any reasonable Invariantist options aside from the four views presented in this chapter. As a result, in order to counter the argument for (I3), I need to reject (J1). This is a problem for me as well, since the goal of this chapter was to argue for Nihilism by showing that the other Invariantist positions are false. The goal of the remainder of this chapter is to show two things. First, I intend to show that a Radicalist cannot have any principled reason to accept (J1).

[39] How much depends on the view. Buchanan (2012) argues that propositional radicals can even be the contents of what are standardly taken to be propositional attitudes (such as belief).

Second, I intend to show that there are some principled reasons to reject Radicalism in favour of Nihilism. As a result, I intend to show that Radicalism is false, regardless of whether Nihilism is true.

Most of the objections against Nihilism are also objections against Radicalism, and most objections against Radicalism are also objections against Nihilism. This is because some of the unpalatable consequences of Nihilism (i.e., we often don't believe the contents of the sentences we utter, even when uttering them sincerely; most of the sentences we utter are false) turn out to be consequences of Radicalism as well (i.e., we often don't believe the contents of the sentences we utter, even when uttering them sincerely; most of the sentences we utter are *untrue*).[40, 41] What I can do in this chapter is to show that the arguments that a Radicalist can give for (J1) are unsound. In other words, there is no sound argument against Nihilism which has only premises that the Radicalist will accept. In particular, I will focus on one argument, which can be summarized with the following thoughts:

> In the Radicalist picture, the propositional radical that our sentences semantically encode acts as a map for the propositions that we intend to communicate. The thought is that, in a context, the proposition that we intend to communicate when we utter (S1) (which is not the proposition that our sentence encodes) is a proposition that has the semantic content of (S1), but fills in the missing relatum.[42] As a result, the Radicalist has a tight connection between the semantic content of our sentences and what we intend to communicate by them. The Nihilist does not have such a connection. The proposition semantically encoded by our utterances of (S1) does not have the semantic content of the proposition that we intend to communicate, since the predicate in (S1) fails to denote any property or relation. As a result, we lose the connection between the proposition semantically encoded by our sentence and the proposition which our sentences intend to

[40] Unless Buchanan (2012) is right. See n.29

[41] On the Radicalist view, the sentences do undergo a level of pragmatic enrichment which leaves them as full propositions.

[42] I am assuming that there is only one proposition that we intend to communicate when we utter (S1). This is not the case, but I hope that the reader will forgive this assumption for the sake of simplicity in exposition. More details on my account of communication will be given in Chapter 3.

communicate. Using some language from Soames (forthcoming), Nihilists must reject that the semantic content of our sentences, together with the context of utterance, determines the proposition we intend to communicate. But we *should* think that the semantic content of our sentences, together with the context of utterance, determines the proposition we intend to communicate.

We can formalize the argument as follows:

(K1) The Semantic content of our sentences, together with the context of utterance, determines the proposition that we intend to communicate.

(K2) If (K1), then Nihilism is false.

(K3) So, Nihilism is false.

In responding to this argument, I will argue that either (K2) or (K1) is false. The reason I will only argue for the disjunction is that arguing directly against (K2) or (K1) would require me to make some assumptions that I would like to avoid. The reason for this is that I believe the following argument to be sound:

(L1) Either Fregeanism about propositions is true, or Russellianism about propoisitions is true.

(L2) If Fregeanism about propositions is true, then (K2) is false.

(L3) If Russellianism about propositions is true, then either (K1) is false or (K2) is false.

(L4) So, either (K1) is false or (K2) is false.

The reason why I won't argue for which of (K1) and (K2) is false is that this is not the place to settle the dispute between Fregeans and neo-Rusellians[43]. I will also not do much in terms of arguing for (L1). I take it that there are many accounts of propositions that differ from the Fregean and the Russellian, but I believe that most of them will fit into one of the two for the relevant parts of my argument.[44] If they do not, I welcome the challenge. As a result, I will focus on arguing for (L2) and

[43] Fregeanism and neo-Russellianism are both described in footnotes 4 and 6 of Chapter 1. Neo-Russellianism is also described in section 1.4.

[44] There are two accounts of propositions that I am ignoring completely: propositions as sets of possible worlds, and propositions as unstructured abstracta (see my footnote 3 in Chapter 1). The reason for this is mostly simplicity. I believe

(L3).

In arguing for (L2), assume that Fregeanism about propositions is true. If this is the case, then the semantic content of predicates is not the property that those predicates denote (if any). If this is so, then there is no reason to think that different non-denoting predicates can't have different semantic content. But if it is possible for different non-denoting predicates to have different semantic content, then it is possible for the semantic content of non-denoting predicates in the sentence which was uttered to be sufficiently similar to the constituents of the proposition which was communicated. An example may clarify this point: According to a standard Fregean theory, the proposition expressed by the sentence "Graham Priest is tall" has as its constituents the sense of "Graham Priest" and the sense of "is tall". Even if "is tall" fails to denote a property (as is the case in Nihilism), the predicate "is tall" may still have a sense.[45] This sense may be different from the sense of the predicate "is strong", even if this predicate also fails to denote a property. So the sentence "Graham Priest is tall", according to the Fregean, has different semantic content than the sentence "Graham Priest is strong", even on the assumption that Nihilism is true. But if that is the case, then there is no reason for us to think that Nihilism is incompatible with the claim that the semantic content of our sentences, together with the context, determines the proposition we intend to communicate. But (K2) claims that Nihilism *is* incompatible with this claim. So, on the assumption that Fregeanism is true, (K2) is false. So (L2) is true.

In order to argue for (L3), assume that Russellianism is true. Then the semantic content of all non-denoting predicates is the same (in that they all lack semantic content). But, independently of the debate regarding context-sensitivity, we should think that there are some predicates that do not denote a property. Consider for example the following speech, inspired by Caplan (2002) and Braun (2005):

---

that the main thought behind my argument will still apply if one of these views is correct.

[45] A Fregean who accepts something like the picture offered by Evans (1982) may reject this, and say that non-denoting terms lack a sense. Other Fregeans may find that any objections to a monadic property of tallness are also objections to a sense of a monadic property of tallness. If this is right, then these Fregeans still need an answer to issues regarding empty names that I present for the Russellian. Whatever response is available to the Russellian should also be available to this kind of Fregean.

> "Let 'Bob' name the thing which is essentially a king of France, if there is one, and nothing otherwise. Let 'Mary' name the thing which is essentially the queen of France, if there is one, and nothing otherwise. Let the predicate 'is Bobbing' denote the property of BEING-IDENTICAL-TO-BOB if there is one, and nothing otherwise. Let the predicate 'is Marying' denote the property of BEING-IDENTICAL-TO-MARY if there is one, and nothing otherwise. Now: Something is Bobbing. Something is Marying."

On the assumption that the speaker is being sincere, and following standard conversational rules, we should think that the sentence "Something is Bobbing" is intended to communicate something different than the sentence "Something is Marying". But, given that there is nothing which is essentially a king of France, and there is nothing which is essentially a queen of France, then there is no property of BEING-IDENTICAL-TO-BOB, and there is no property of BEING-IDENTICAL-TO-MARY. So neither the predicate "is Bobbing" nor the predicate "is Marying" denote a property. So on the Russellian picture, the semantic content of both of these sentences is the same.

The Russellian has two options here. On the one hand, she can claim that it is not the case that the semantic content of the two sentences above, plus the context of utterance, determine the propositions that the speaker intended to communicate. This would be to reject (K1). On the other hand, the Russellian could accept (K1) and claim that the context is sufficiently robust to force the two sentences above to communicate different propositions. Suppose the Russellian takes this option. Then there is no reason to think that the Russellian wouldn't also take this option when it comes to context-sensitive predicates. There doesn't seem to be a significant difference between the two types of cases: they are cases where we understand that the speaker intends to communicate different propositions by uttering different sentences, even though the semantic content of those sentences is the same. So a Russellian that takes this second option would have no reason to think that Nihilism is incompatible with the claim that the semantic content of an uttered sentence, plus the context of utterance, determines the proposition that the speaker intended to communicate. This would amount to rejecting

(K2). I take it that there are no other options for the Russellian here[46]. As a result, under the assumption that Russellianism is true, either (K1) is false, or (K2) is false. More details on how the Russellian can explain communication in a Nihilist context will be given in Chapter 3.

I now ask the reader to allow me to indulge in a bit of conjecture: I believe that there are no other arguments against Nihilism that only have premises that a Radicalist will accept. This allows me to construct the following argument against Radicalism:

(M1) Nihilism has all the theoretical virtues that Radicalism has, but fewer theoretical vices.[47]

(M2) If (M1), then Radicalism is false.

(M3) So, Radicalism is false.

(M1) is really a challenge to the proponent of Radicalism. Given that (K1)-(K3) is unsound, I challenge the Radicalist to come up with a theoretical virtue of Radicalism that the Nihilist cannot also capture. Some of the theoretical vices that Radicalism has, but Nihilism avoids, are as follows. Nihilism is more qualitatively ontologically parsimonious than Radicalism, since it has no need for the ontological kind *propositional radical.* It is also simpler, since it offers a non-disjunctive account of what syntactically correct English sentences express. Radicalism captures our intuition that sentences like "Graham Priest is tall" are about tallness, but Nihilism captures our intuitions that sentences like "Graham Priest is tall" have truth values.[48] Both views can find ways to explain away these intuitions by appealing to

[46] This is not completely right. The Russellian in question could make the Meinongian move and claim that there is a property of *being identical to Bob*, and there is a property of *being identical to Mary.* On this view, the semantic content of the two sentences above is in fact different. The only thing I can say in response to this is that versions of Meinongianism that allow a Russellian to make this claim are extremely problematic (but see Priest, 2005). A more moderate Russellian may claim that, although there are no such properties as those denoted in the speech above, but that context-sensitive predicates are disanalogous: they do express some property (or relation, etc.). While this move allows the Russellian to avoid my argument, it begs the question against the Nihilist. The claim made in (K2) was that Nihilism is incompatible with (K1), not that Nihilism is false.

[47] This criterion is only added to avoid counterexamples of the form "Radicalism is true; so, Nihilism is false." or "x is true; so Nihilism is false" where x is some consequence of Radicalism that is just as in need of justification as Radicalism itself (such as 'context-sensitive predicates denote a relation' or 'context-sensitive sentences don't express propositions'). I don't mean anything stronger than that by 'non-question-begging.'

[48] Chris Tillman has mentioned to me that there is a tendency among neo-Russellians to take "aboutness" intuitions more seriously than "truth-value" intuitions. I'm inclined to agree that this is true, but I think it is a bad idea. Taking aboutness intuitions so seriously has led Russellians to highly inflaitonary ontologies, including not only fictional and mythical creatures, but also non-existing objects (see, for example, Salmon 1998).I discuss these kinds of neo-Russellian views in 3.3.

pragmatics (more on this in Chapter 3), so I take it that it is a tie on intuitive plausibility. On other virtues, it seems that Nihilism and Radicalism are on par.

My justification for (M2) is as follows. Assume (M1) is truc. Then either the vices of Nihilism and Radicalism are sufficient to defeat both theories, or they are not. If the first disjunct is true, then Radicalism is false (and so is Nihilism). If the second disjunct is true, then the only reason we might prefer Radicalism over Nihilism is because of some theoretical virtue. But, via (M1), Radicalism is less theoretically virtuous than Nihilism. So, in the absence of new problems for Nihilism that don't have a parallel for Radicalism, we should think that Radicalism is false. Informally, if as Nihilism beats Radicalism in simplicity and parsimony, and ties it in everything else, then, regardless of whether Nihilism is true, we should think that Radicalism is false. So, on the assumption that Nihilism has all the same theoretical virtues that Radicalism does, but fewer vices, we should think that Radicalism is false. So, we should think that (M2) is true.

2.4 Conclusion:

In this chapter, I have presented what I take to be the four different versions of Invariantism in conceptual space. I have argued that Property Invariantism, whether Restricted or Minimal, fails to account for why our predicates pick out the properties that the Property Invariantist claims that they do. I have furthermore argued that the Property Invariantist view is unmotivated, as we gain no explanatory benefits by accepting the existence of these properties. I have also argued that, as long as there is no motivation for Radicalism that is not also motivation for Nihilism, Radicalism is a less reasonable view to hold than Nihilism. Since I take these four versions to exhaust our options for Invariantism, and I take myself to have argued successfully for the truth of Invariantism in Chapter 1, I conclude that, short of any objections to Nihilism, we have good reasons to believe that Nihilism is true. In Chapter 3, I will try to respond to objections to Nihilism, especially those arising from coupling Nihilism with a neo-Russellian theory of propositions. I believe that these are the only serious problems left for the Nihilist to respond to. If I respond to them successfully, I believe I will have made a strong case for the truth of Invariantist Nihilism.

Chapter 3: Defending Nihilism

3.0 Introduction

In Chapter 2, I argued that versions of Invariantism other than Nihilism have serious problems. Together with my arguments for the truth of Invariantism in Chapter 1, this should give us a case for the truth of Invariantist Nihilism. There are, however, some problems with invariantist Nihilism. The main issue with Nihilism is that, since almost all terms are apparently context sensitive, then almost all terms fail to pick out properties. So Nihilism appears to be committed to the claim that almost no English predicate denotes any property. In the first section of this chapter, I will explore why exactly we might think that this constitutes an *objection* to Nihilism. I hope to show that if Cappelen and Lepore's objection to Nihilism is correct, it is because Nihilism is incompatible with another view about semantic content: neo-Russellianism. I will then spend the remainder of this chapter arguing that, on every alleged instance of incompatibility between Nihilism and neo-Russellianism, these two views are in fact compatible.

3.1 "Metaphysical" Nihilism:

According to Cappelen and Lepore, Metaphysical Nihilism is the view that "the entire idea that two things can have the same properties or engage in the same activities is doubtful" (2005, p.163). Cappelen and Lepore also describe Metaphysical Nihilism as the view that "whatever worries there are about [being tall] generalize to everything". There are two ways to read this account of Metaphysical Nihilism. On one version, Metaphysical Nihilism is the view that for any two things, there is no property that those two things have in common. This is a claim about the metaphysics of properties. I argued in Chapter 2 that there is no reason to think that Metaphysical Nihilism follows from the rejection of a property of BEING-TALL. A second way to understand Metaphysical Nihilism is the claim that for any predicate in English, that predicate fails to express a property or relation. This is a semantic view, and should really be labeled "*Semantic* Nihilism".[49] Semantic Nihilism is consistent both with the truth and falsity of Metaphysical Nihilism, since it is quite possible that there be some properties that no linguistic terms denote, while no linguistic term denotes any property. As a result, although I argued against Metaphysical Nihilism in Chapter 2, I have not yet considered the argument that Invariantist Nihilism is committed to Semantic Nihilism. I explore a version of Cappelen and Lepore's argument for this conclusion in this section.

Cappelen and Lepore argue that any view other than Minimalism is committed to Semantic Nihilism. Their argument, as it applies to "is tall", is as follows. Suppose we think, as I have argued, that there is no such thing as the property of BEING-TALL. The reason we think this is because tallness is a relation, and one which requires a comparison class. But the same kinds of intuitions that lead us to think that there is no such property as BEING-TALL would also lead us to think that there is no such relation as BEING-TALL-WITH-RESPECT-TO. For consider the sentence "Graham Priest is tall in comparison to the average human". This sentence also seems incomplete when discussing *how* the comparison is to be made:

> Graham Priest is tall in comparison to most humans when standing on his tip-toes;
>
> Graham Priest is tall in comparison to most humans when most humans are stretching but Priest isn't;
>
> Graham Priest is tall in comparison to most humans when measured from his ankles to his neck;

and so on. The thought that Cappelen and Lepore have is that this should lead us to think that there is no such thing as the relation of BEING-TALL-WITH-RESPECT-TO, any more than we should think that there is a property of BEING-TALL. But, with enough creativity, we can construct these kinds of

---

[49] Unfortunately, the term 'Semantic Nihilism' has been used by Braun and Sider (2007) to describe a view slightly different from this one. According to Braun and Sider, semantic nihilism is the view that any sentences containing vague predicates are neither true nor false because they fail to encode a single proposition. 'Semantic Nihilism' as I am using it, is a slightly different view: it is the view that all sentences have some predicate that does not pick out any property. Semantic Nihilism, here, is neutral on whether the sentences are false or merely untrue. The view I am arguing for, however, does insist that these sentences would be false.

examples for any candidate property or relation. So we should think that for any predicate, no matter how complex it is, there is no corresponding property. But this cannot be right. So views that reject the existence of a property of BEING-TALL (which is almost all views except for Minimal Property Invariantism) are false as well. Since Invariantist Nihilism rejects the existence of a property of BEING-TALL, this argument affects Nihilism as well. Formalized, I see the argument as follows:

(A1) If Nihilism is true, then there is no property of BEING-TALL.

(A2) If there is no property of BEING-TALL, then for any predicate P in English, P fails to denote.

(A3) It is not the case that, for any predicate P in English, P fails to denote.

(A4) So, Nihilism is false.

Cappelen and Lepore's main support for (A2) is their claim that a person that is creative enough, could make us doubt the existence of any property by coming up with clever situations of context-sensitivity. I believe that there are ways to avoid this kind of objection. The most promising, I think, is to claim that our intuitions about the naturalness of certain properties can allow us to explain why some predicates pick out properties and some don't. I also believe that whether a predicate is vulnerable to Cappelen and Lepore's argument will depend on how that predicate was introduced into the language. Finally, I think certain logical and mathematical predicates may be invulnerable to the type of arguments I gave for the non-existence of BEING-TALL. But I would like to bracket these responses and focus on a different way of rejecting Cappelen and Lepore's argument: denying (A3). For the remainder of this chapter, then, I will accept that if there is no property of BEING-TALL, then not a single predicate in English picks out any property.

Cappelen and Lepore accept (A3), but they do not give much of an argument for why. Part of the reason is that they find the claim that no predicates pick out properties implausible. I can't argue against what seems plausible or implausible, but I can make the following point: once we've accepted any version of Invariantism, we are going to arrive at apparently implausible results about the content and truth values of our sentences, so we'd better get used to it. Another reason Cappelen and Lepore may have for thinking that (A3) is true is that they think that the burden of proof is on the denier of (A3), and that the denier of (A3) has no arguments for his thesis. But the denier of (A3) *does* have an argument in his favour: there is no property of BEING-TALL, and Invariantism is true! I believe my discussion in Chapter 2 has met the burden of proof that was required of me. So Cappelen and Lepore owe us an argument for why (A3) is true. I hope to offer some on their behalf, and reply to them.

Why would we think of some predicate that it picks out a property? One reason would be if we think that sentences that have this predicate are *true*. If sentences that have the predicate are true, then the property picked out by the predicate is instantiated by the individual picked out by the subject. So there is a property picked out by the predicate. Unfortunately, Cappelen and Lepore don't have this argument available to them, and neither do Minimalists or Radicalists. This is because, as argued in 2.2 and 2.3, our intuitions about whether sentences are *true* are highly unreliable according to these views (see Cappelen and Lepore, 2005).

A second reason for thinking that some predicate picks out a property is if picking out that property plays an important role in communication. If the predicate did not pick out a property, then some facts about communication would be unexplained. I believe that this objection only really applies when Nihilism is conjoined with another popular view about semantic content: neo-Russelianism. As a result, I will spend most of this chapter arguing that neo-Russelianism and Nihilism are perfectly compatible, and can give an adequate account of communication.

A third reason to think that at least *some* predicates pick out properties is that if they did not, then semantic content would be explanatorily irrelevant, and we should cease to believe in it. This is a version of an objection raised by Robyn Carston (2002) and Francois Recanati (2004). I will spend the final section of this chapter addressing this last issue.

If these are all the available reasons for accepting (A3), then I believe I have a counter to every one of them. As a result, Cappelen and Lepore's objection to Nihilism fails. In the process, I intend to show that some other natural objections to Nihilism fail as well.

3.2 Neo-Russellian Propositions: Recall that what I call neo-Russellianism is the conjunction of the following theses:

(I) The semantic content of a name, if any, is the object it refers to, if any.

(II) The semantic content of a predicate, if any, is the property or relation that it expresses, if any.

(III) The semantic content of a sentence, if any, is a structured proposition.

(IV) The semantic contents of names and predicates in a sentence are the constituents of the proposition expressed by that sentence.

(V) Some expressions have semantic content.

In this chapter, neo-Russelian propositions will be depicted as ordered n-tuples that have as elements the properties, relations and objects that are constituents of those propositions. For simple one-place properties, the schema will be <*property*, *object*>, while for relations, the schema will be <n-place relation, <object$_1$,..., object$_n$>>. More complex propositions will follow iterations of the schema above. I omit quantified expressions for the sake of simplicity. This is not to say that neo-Russellian propositions are ordered n-tuples; there are good reasons to think that they are not (Soames, et al., 2014, Ch. 3). The n-tuple representation of propositions is not intended as a presentation of what the propositions actually are. I remain agnostic with regards to the question of what propositions are. Hence, the Minimalist neo-Russellian proposition expressed by "Graham Priest is tall" can be represented as:

(B1) <BEING-TALL, Graham Priest>

For the corresponding Radicalist neo-Russelian propositional radical, there are two options:

(B2) <BEING-TALL-WITH-RESPECT-TO, <Graham Priest, ________>>

(B3) <BEING-TALL-WITH-RESPECT-TO, Graham Priest>

There are important consequences regarding which of the above we think best represents the Radicalist position. There are two reasons for this: first, (B2) is a gappy proposition, while (B3) is not. This is relevant because, as I will argue, gappy propositions such as (B2) do have truth values, and can be contents of propositional attitudes, and are therefore best thought of as full-fledged propositions, Second, the structure of (B3) corresponds to the sentence structure of "Graham Priest is tall", while the structure of (B2) does not. This is because "Graham Priest is tall" has a subject term and a one-place predicate. (B3) has a "slot" for a one-place property, while (B2) has a "slot" for a two-place relation.[50] This is relevant because many Invariantist arguments favour the view that propositional structure should tend to mirror sentence structure.[51]

The Nihilist proposition I have in mind can be represented by neo-Russellians as:

(B4) <_______, Graham Priest>

Given the picture above, an immediate objection to neo-Russelian Nihilism comes to mind. (B2) and (B4) are missing a constituent. Call these alleged propositions that are missing constituents "gappy propositions". The argument is as follows: there are no gappy propositions. But Nihilism requires the existence of gappy propositions. So Nihilism is false. Formally:

(C1) There are no gappy propositions.

(C2) If there are no gappy propositions, then Nihilism is false.

(C3) So, Nihilism is false.

---

[50]One might worry that my talk of "slots" is merely metaphorical, and that (B2) and (B3) are just different schemas for the same entity. But talk of "slots" cannot be understood as *merely* metaphorical, since it is essential to distinguishing propositions. Consider the IS-A PART OF relation, which can take any number of relata equal to or greater than 2. Let 'a' and 'b' name two arbitrary objects, let 'c' be a non-denoting term, and let 'P' express the IS-A PART OF relation. I think that it is clear that 'Pcab' and 'Pab' express two different propositions. But this can only be the case if we take "slots" seriously, schematizing the propositions expressed respectively as

(b1) <IS-A PART OF, <__, a, b>>

(b2) <IS-A PART OF, <a, b>>

This should give us good reasons to think that "slots" talk is not merely metaphorical, and that the entities purportedly denoted by (B2) and (B3) are distinct.

[51]See Cappelen and Lepore (2005)

Note that (C1) does not state that gappy propositions are just propositional radicals. This is a weaker claim that I will argue against later. The stronger claim here is that there just are no entities such as (B2) and (B4). The argument that gappy propositions do not exist has been most recently made by Mousavian (2011). Mousavian claims that the only parts of a proposition are its constituents. But if this is right, then the gappy proposition expressed by (B4) is an object that has Graham Priest as a part, and no other parts. But the only object that has Graham Priest as a part, and no further parts, is Graham Priest. So, if there are gappy propositions, then Graham Priest is a gappy proposition. Furthermore, there could be double-gappy propositions, propositions that are missing both the predicate-slot constituent and their subject-slot constituent.[52] All it takes is for someone to utter the sentence that has the non-denoting name as the subject and the non-denoting predicate as the object. But double-gappy propositions, since they have no constituents, *have no parts*. But that would mean that there are no double-gappy propositions.

It is hard to respond to Mousavian on this issue without getting too involved in the logic of parthood, or in the metaphysics of propositions, both of which would require a longer treatment than I can give. Hopefully this response will suffice: as far as I am aware, it is not necessary for a Russellian to accept that propositions have parts, and many Russellians remain agnostic about this issue. Furthermore, Russellians that do accept that propositions have parts find themselves in need to reject some posits of classical extensional mereology.[53] So, the Russellians that accept that propositions have parts have ways of dealing with Mousavian's argument, while the Russellians that reject that propositions have parts are unaffected by it..

So there are no good arguments against the existence of gappy propositions, independently of arguments against Russellianism generally. But are there any reasons, independently of Nihilism, to

[52] This is certainly the case if Nihilism is true. Consider Plato's assertion that all properties instantiate themselves. Plato might then have said "*being tall* is tall". If Nihilism is true, then Plato's sentence expresses a double-gappy proposition. Even without Nihilism, if there is at least one non-denoting name and one non-denoting predicate, then there is at least one double-gappy proposition.

[53] See Keller, forthcoming; Tillman and Fowler (2012). For further discussion of whether a Russellian should understand constituents as parts, see Caplan and Tillman (ms),

believe that there *are* gappy propositions? When arguing against Radicalism, I claimed that one advantage of Nihilism is that it does not need to posit any new category of object. So it is important for me to demonstrate that neo-Russelians already have reasons to believe in gappy propositions. The main reason to think that there are gappy propositions is that people can both assert and believe, for example, that Pegasus is a flying horse. Le Verrier honestly believed that Vulcan orbited the Sun. But neither Pegasus nor Vulcan exist.[54] So, if Le Verrier honestly believed that Vulcan orbited the Sun, and neo-Russelianism is true, then Le Verrier believed the proposition <ORBITING, <______, Sun>>. So, independently of Nihilism, there are already good reasons to believe that there are gappy propositions.

A weaker argument against Nihilism is as follows: what I have been calling "gappy propositions" is just another name for what Radicalists call "propositional radicals." This is because gappy propositions, as well as propositional radicals, are both devoid of truth values. So Nihilism is really just a version of Radicalism.

At first pass, this cannot be right. Radicalists argue that propositional radicals cannot be the objects of propositional attitudes. Bach (1997) is a Radicalist who argues that we do not in fact believe what our sentences say, even when we utter them sincerely. So either Bach is wrong about what propositional radicals are, or propositional radicals are not gappy propositions. This tilts the scale more heavily towards (B3) as an interpretation of what propositional radicals might be. But there is a bigger problem with this objection: gappy propositions don't lack truth values. As Braun (2005) has argued, there are reasons to think that gappy propositions do have truth values. This is because the sentence "Pegasus does not exist" is true and can be represented as the Russellian proposition <Negation, <EXISTING, ______>>. So, Braun argues, negated gappy propositions certainly appear to be true. That should lead us to think that "Pegasus exists" is false. But then there is a gappy proposition which is

---

[54] Even if Pegasus and Vulcan do exist as mythical objects, it is unlikely that the words "Pegasus" and "Vulcan" have always been used to refer to such objects. See Braun (2005).

false. So gappy propositions are not just propositional radicals. This is because they can be the contents of propositional attitudes, and because they have truth values.[55]

A possible reply here is that it is not the Nihilist but the Radicalist who has been wrong. Radicalists mistakenly thought that propositional radicals lacked truth values and could not be content of propositional attitudes. But propositional radicals *can* have truth values, and they can be the content of propositional attitudes. So Nihilism and Radicalism are still the same view after all.

This picture is compatible only with the radicalist that translates "Graham Priest is tall" as (B2)

(B2) <BEING-TALL -WITH-RESPECT-TO, <Graham Priest, _______>>.

Supposing that this is in fact the Radicalist's view, I accept the objection. It turns out that the Radicalists have been Nihilists all along. Not only that, they have been *bad* Nihilists. (B2), unlike (B4), does not respect the structure of the sentence "Graham Priest is tall." In fact, (B2) makes "Graham Priest is tall" synonymous with "Graham Priest is tall with respect to Pegasus." While Russellians are used to accepting that two sentences with different words might express the same proposition, I have yet to see an argument for thinking that two sentences with a different *quantity of singular terms* can express the same proposition.[56] So the interpretation of gappy propositions in which they are just propositional radicals would make Radicalists **very** wrong. I would rather be more charitable to Radicalists, and interpret them as translating "Graham Priest is tall" as (B3):

(B3) <BEING-TALL-WITH-RESPECT-TO, Graham Priest>

As a result, we can now have a coherent neo-Russellian Nihilist picture of the semantic content of context-sensitive terms. The sentence "Graham Priest is tall" expresses that false gappy proposition depicted by (B4):

(B4) <______, Graham Priest>.

---

[55] Some philosophers who have argued that gappy propositions *cannot* have truth values include Salmon (1998), and Adams et. al. (2002)

[56] A hard case here are the sentences "Russell believed logicism" and "Russell believed that arithmetic reduces to logic," since they appear to express the same proposition. But this is because "that logic reduces to arithmetic" functions in the sentence above as a singular term that denotes a proposition. We have no such case in the sentences offered in the main text.

3.3 Neo-Russellian Permissivism:

Among neo-Russellians, it has become more common to accept the existence of fictional, imaginary, and even mythical characters. According to these views, although there are no winged horses, Pegasus exists as a mythical creature; although there are no wizards, Harry Potter exists as a fictional character. These fictional, imaginary and mythical objects don't have the properties that are attributed to them. Although Harry Potter exists, *it* is not a wizard; it is some abstract artifact created by J.K Rowling; although Pegasus exists, it is not a horse; it is an abstract object created by some ancient Greeks (Salmon 1998, Braun 2005). Although this view is not unique to neo-Russellians, it does provide the neo-Russellian a special benefit. If there were no Pegasus and there were no Harry Potter, then the sentences "Pegasus flies" and "Harry Potter flies" would express the same neo-Russellian gappy proposition. The neo-Russellian Permissivist incurs the cost of including more entities into her ontology to get the benefit of a more intuitively plausible account of the content of the two sentences above.

I do not intend to settle the question of whether there are fictional or mythical entities. Rather, I'm interrested in an option that is available to the neo-Russellian Permissivist with regards to the debate in question. A neo-Russellian who is inclined to accept the existence of mythical and fictional creatures may be more inclined to accept the existence of the fictional or mythical property of BEING-TALL. The resulting view would be somewhat similar to Invariantist Nihilism: although there is no property of BEING-TALL, there is a mythical/fictional/imaginary property of tallness, and it is the semantic content of the predicate "is tall". It is not clear whether this mythical property of tallness is itself actually a property, or only fictionally so. If the mythical property is not a property, then the view is a version of Invariantist Nihilism. If the mythical property is a property, then the view is a strange view between Invariantist Nihilism and some sort of Property Minimalism, where the property of BEING-TALL is a mythical property that no existing object has.

I think that both of these options are in the spirit of Invariantist Nihilism, so I don't see much of a reason to argue against them. One thing I would like to note is that the alleged mythical property of tallness is not like any fictional, imaginary or mythical object in that *almost no speakers have imagined it*. Some theorists may have created the mythical property of tallness over the last few decades (when discussions of minimal properties begun), but speakers have been using the predicate "is tall" for much longer than that without thinking that there is a monadic property of tallness. This is not intended to be a conclusive objection, but it is a worry for applying the Russellian Permissivist strategy to Invariantist Nihilism.

3.4 Objections to Neo-Russellian Nihilism

I believe that there are three main objections to the compatibility between neo-Russellianism and Nihilism. The first objection is as follows. Most speakers, presumably, don't believe (B4).

(B4) <______, Graham Priest>.

Speakers may say, however, that Graham Priest is tall and be sincere while doing so. As a result, we are forced to conclude that speakers sometimes utter a sentence sincerely without believing the content of that sentence. But this is implausible, since uttering a sentence sincerely involves committing oneself to what that sentence says. The, argument, then, is:

(C1) If Nihilism and neo-Russellianism are both true, then sometimes competent speakers will sincerely say something that they do not believe.

(C2) Competent speakers never sincerely say something that they do not believe.

(C3) So, Nihilism and neo-Russellianism are not both true.

A second objection to the conjunction of Nihilism and neo-Russellianism is the following. If Nihilism and neo-Russellianism are both true, then "Graham Priest is tall" and Graham Priest is smart" express the same Russellian Proposition, namely (B4).

(B4) <______, Graham Priest>.

But the two sentences above are used to communicate very different information. The Nihilist, unlike the Minimalist and the Radicalist, doesn't have any story to tell about why this is so. The objection, then, is:

(D1) If Nihilism and neo-Russellianism are both true, then two sentences with different context-sensitive predicates express the same proposition.

(D2) If two sentences with different context-sensitive predicates express the same proposition, then there is no explanation for why two sentences with different context-sensitive predicates communicate different information.

(D3) There is an explanation for why two sentences with different context-sensitive predicates communicate different information.

(D4) So, Nihilism and neo-Russellianism are not both true.

The third and final objection to the conjunction of neo-Russellianism and Nihilism regards the explanatory value of semantic content. If neo-Russellianism and Nihliism are both true, then almost all communication happens at the level of pragmatics, while semantic content does very little to no explanatory work. If this is right, however, then there is no reason for us to believe that there is such a thing as semantic content in the first place. The objection, then, is:

(E1) If Nihilsm and neo-Russellianism are both true, then semantic content plays no role in explaining communication.

(E2) If semantic content plays no role in explaining communication, then there is no such thing as semantic content.

(E3) If there is no such thing as semantic content, then neo-Russellianism is false.

(E4) So, Nihilism and neo-Russellianism are not both true.

I believe that all three of these objections are unsound. More specifically, I deny (C2), (D2), and both (E1) and (E2) in the above arguments. My reasons for denying these premises, however, require me to engage in an extensive discussion of Invariantist accounts of communication, especially those given by neo-Russellians. The way this section will be structured is as follows: I will assume neo-Russellianism. I will then provide a basic account of the relation between semantic content and communication on this neo-Russellian picture. The account will be heavily based on the work of Scott Soames (forthcoming) and David Braun (2012). First, I will show how every invariantist is committed to the falsity of (D2). This does not mean that (D2) is false, but it means that the objection (D) is not unique to Nihilism. Given that Invariantism generally is independently well-motivated, we have good reasons to reject (D2) anyway. Following this, I will show how the standard account of communication can be extended to a Nihilist account, thereby giving me the resources to deny (C2). I will then assess the objection (E) in more detail, by examining similar arguments given by Recanati (2004) and Carston (2002). I will then show why both (E1) and (E2) are false. Short of any other objections to neo-Russellian Nihlism, I will conclude that the conjunction of Nihilism and neo-Russellianism is perfectly compatible.

3.5 The Basic Picture of Communication:

When we utter a sentence like "Graham Priest is tall", there are three classes of propositions that are importantly related to that utterance. First, there is the class of propositions that are said. These are going to be the propositions that our "says-that" reports capture. Second, there is the class of propositions that are asserted. These are the propositions that the speaker intends listeners to understand by the utterance "Graham Priest is tall". This is a bit unclear now, but I will give a more precise account of assertion later. Third, there is the proposition that is the semantic content of the utterance "Graham Priest is tall". This, borrowing a term from Braun (2012), can be called the proposition *locuted*.

An interesting question to ask, at this point, is what the relationship is between these three classes of propositions. A tempting picture is the following:

(i) When we utter "Graham Priest is tall" in a context C, we locute a single proposition.

(ii) The proposition locuted belongs to the class of propositions that are asserted in C.

(iii) Any sentence that obviously logically follows in C from the proposition locuted belongs to the class of the propositions asserted in C.

(iv) No other propositions are asserted by an utterance of "Graham Priest is tall" in C.

(v) What is said in C just is what is asserted in C.

If Invariantism (of any kind) is true, however, it would follow from this picture that not only is semantic content invariant, but what is asserted and what is said are both invariant as well. For if Invariantism is true, then the proposition locuted by by "Graham Priest is tall" is the same in all contexts. What obviously logically follows from this proposition the same in all contexts (assuming that the listeners are all equally competent at logic). So, according to the picture above, what is asserted by "Graham Priest is tall" is the same in all contexts in which speakers are equally competent at logic. This is a problem, since it blocks a tempting explanation of how Invariantist communication works: although we locute the same proposition in all contexts, we often assert different propositions with it.

Note that the need to reject (i)-(v) is a problem for Invariantism generally, and no mention of either neo-Russellianism nor Nihilism has been made. The real problem shows up when we look at what neo-Russelian Invariantists say in order to reject the picture above. I will mainly focus on the work of Soames and Braun, although some mention will also be made of Cappelen and Lepore. The standard picture of communication that they have in mind is as follows: semantic content is not always asserted (reject ii). Semantic content, however, determines what is asserted by going through a process of enrichment, where the context takes in semantic content and outputs the asserted propositions. (iii) and (iv) are true when adjusted to be about the propositions asserted after enrichment, rather than the proposition locuted. There is some disagreement about the truth of (v), and I will say more about this in 3.7.

Soames agrees in spirit with (i), even though he thinks that what is locuted is a propositional radical that has no truth conditions. Braun agrees with (i) simpliciter, since he is a Minimalist.[57] The rest of the picture is one that Soames and Braun either reject outright or accept only with some qualifications. One of the main insights of the Soames and Braun picture is to show that (ii) is false: sometimes, the proposition locuted by our sentences fails to be part of what is asserted. I will look at some examples in the following section.

3.6 Soames' Picture of Semantic Content:

Soames (forthcoming) presents a picture of semantic content that is intended to be compatible with Invariantism. In Soames' Radicalist picture, the semantic content of a sentence such as "Graham Priest is tall" is a propositional skeleton of the form <BEING-TALL-WITH-RESPECT-TO, Graham Priest>, which fails to have a truth value due to its incompleteness.[58] In a context, however, the propositional skeleton above undergoes a process of *pragmatic enrichment*. Basically, the conversational context, combined with the propositional skeleton, gives us a complete proposition. In this case, the complete proposition would include the contextually relevant comparison class C, and give us a proposition of the form <BEING-TALL-WITH-RESPECT-TO, <Graham Priest, C>>. This pragmatically enriched proposition, Soames says, is a proposition asserted in context C. This proposition, plus all and only the propositions that are "relevant, unmistakable, necessary and apriori consequences of the speaker's primary assertions, together with salient presuppositions of the conversational background"

[57]This is not completely right, since Braun thinks that sentences including vague terms indeterminately encode multiple propositions. As a result, it is sometimes the case that more than one proposition is locuted. If we clarify enough to remove vagueness and ambiguities, then Braun would agree that only one proposition is locuted. See Braun and Sider (2007) for further discussion.

[58]Soames does not say anything specific regarding the predicate "is tall", which he may be a Minimalist (rather than a Radicalist) about. I am using the example only to preserve continuity from previous chapters of this thesis.

(forthcoming, p.5) are the asserted propositions. So, for example, the conjunction of the pragmatically enriched proposition with itself may also count among the asserted propositions.

Soames thinks that it is not only propositional radicals that can undergo a process of pragmatic enrichment, but that propositions can do so too (see Soames 2002).

> When you ask "Were any of your neighbors in Princeton philosophers?", and I answer "yes, Carl Hempel, was my neighbor", what I assert is that the philosopher, Carl Hempel, was my neighbor (p.8)

The thought is that the proposition locuted by "Carl Hempel was my neighbor" is in all contexts in which Soames uses it the proposition that can be expressed by <BEING-A-NEIGHBOUR-OF, <Carl Hempel, Scott Soames>>. But the proposition asserted in the quoted passage is a pragmatically enriched proposition: <BEING-A-NEIGHBOUR-OF, <<Carl Hempel, BEING-A-PHILOSOPHER>, Scott Soames>>. This is because, in the particular context of the quote above, Soames is asserting, not only that Carl Hempel is his neighbor, but also that Carl Hempel is a philosopher. So, on Soames' picture, it is not necessary that the semantic entity that undergoes pragmatic enrichment be a propositional radical.[59]

We can now see how this picture might be extended from a Radicalist view to a Minimalist view. The Minimalist believes that the predicate "is tall" encodes the one-place property of BEING-TALL. As a result, "Graham Priest is tall" semantically encodes the proposition <BEING-TALL, Graham Priest>. Presumably, the asserted proposition will still be the pragmatically enriched proposition <BEING-TALL-WITH-RESPECT-TO, <Graham Priest, C>>. So, as long as pragmatic enrichment can get us from the Minimal proposition to the asserted proposition, Soames' picture works fairly well for the Minimalist as well. How the Minimalist can do this is an interesting question, but I am willing to grant

[59] Braun and Sider (2006) have given really interesting objections to Soames' claim that sentences like "Carl Hempel was my neighbor" go through a process of pragmatic enrichment as described above. Their objections, however, are not objections against pragmatic enrichment generally; they are objections against pragmatic enrichment when it comes to proper names. It is far from clear that these objections would translate well into a discussion of enrichment as I will be discussing it. As a consequence of this, I will put these objections aside.

the Minimalist that she can. So I will assume, for the rest of this chapter, that pragmatic enrichment works well both for the Minimalist and the Radicalist. This is because both the Minimalist and the Radicalist have some proposition, or propositional radical, that is just a less complete version of the proposition that is asserted. So, all pragmatic enrichment needs to do is add a few pieces. Of course, more will need to be said about exactly *how* pragmatic enrichment works, but the picture presented above is intended as a first step.

We now have a coherent Invariantist picture of communication. When someone utters a sentence such as "Graham Priest is tall", what is locuted is the same in all contexts. What the speaker asserts by uttering "Graham Priest is tall", however, will depend on the context. In some contexts, the speaker will assert that Graham Priest is tall with respect to the Oklahoma City Thunder. In other contexts, the speaker will assert that Graham Priest is tall with respect to my 9-year old cousin. Sometimes the assertion made by an utterance of "Graham Priest is tall" will be true, sometimes it will be false. But the semantic content of "Graham Priest is tall", and the truth value of such semantic content, remains invariant.

There are still more questions to be answered, however. First, is it ever the case that what is locuted is *not* among what is asserted? And second, which propositions belong to the class of *what is said*?

3.7 Believing What We Say:

The goal of this section is to show that all versions of invariantism are committed to the claim that what is located is not always asserted. As a result, I will give some reasons for denying premise (C2) in our first argument against neo-Russellian Nihilism:

(C2) Competent speakers never sincerely say something that they do not believe.

I will show that both Minimalists and Radicalists are committed to this claim, and that it is therefore not an extra cost for Nihilists to accept this claim as well.

To show that Radicalists are committed to rejecting that what is locuted is always asserted, we can just ask what kind of objects are candidates for being asserted. The answer, at least the one that is salient from Soames' picture, is that it is only *propositions* that can be asserted. But, as I argued in the previous section, and as the Radicalists so often remind us, propositional radicals are not propositions. So, propositional radicals are never asserted. But according to radicalism propositional radicals are sometimes locuted. So sometimes, what is locuted is not among what is asserted.

To show that Minimalists are committed to the claim that what is locuted is not always asserted, a little bit more work needs to be done. My example, here, will be Braun's (2012) Minimalist theory of "might", but I will use this example to draw more general conclusions. Braun is a Minimalist about "might": he believes that the word "might" singles out the property of BEING-POSSIBLE. This is not the property of BEING-METAPHYSICALLY-POSSIBLE, the property of BEING-EPISTEMICALLY-POSSIBLE, or the property of BEING-NOMICALLY-POSSIBLE. It is the property of BEING-POSSIBLE simpliciter. So the statement:

(F1) Goldbach's conjecture might be true.

Expresses the Minimal proposition

(F2) <BEING-POSSIBLE, <BEING-TRUE, Goldbach's conjecture>>

As a Minimalist, Braun claims that the property of BEING-POSSIBLE is a property that all things that are possible have, as long as they are possible in some way. So (F1) is true if the truth of Goldbach's conjecture is epistemically, but not metaphysically possible, or even if it is metaphysically but not nomically possible. As long as it is possible in at least one way for Goldbach's conjecture to be true, (F1) is true.

The interesting question comes up when we look at sentences about what *must* be true. Consider, then:

(F3) Fermat's last theorem must be true.

I assume that we want to maintain the claim that 'possibly *p'* is logically equivalent to 'not necessarily not *p*'. I also assume that a Minimalist wants to understand the word "must" as picking out the property of BEING-NECESSARY. Given these assumptions, we can show that (F3) is false. This is because it expresses the following proposition:

(F4) <NEGATION <BEING-POSSIBLE, NEGATION<BEING-TRUE, Fermat's last theorem>>>

The reason (F4) is false is because it is, in some context, epistemically possible for Fermat's last theorem to be false. But we can easily consider a situation where a math professor sincerely says "thanks to recent work in mathematics, we now know that Fermat's last theorem must be true". Presumably, our math professor isn't asserting anything false in his statement. But he is locuting (F3), which is false. So, he is not asserting (F3). Presumably, our math professor also does not believe (F3), even if he does believe the pragmatically enriched proposition that he asserted. Therefore, it is possible, on a Minimalist Invariantism, for what is locuted not to be among what is asserted or believed.

So far, I have only discussed the relation between what is locuted, what is asserted and what is believed. I have shown that, according to Invariantism, sometimes what we locute is not among what we assert or believe. But although the objection (C) made reference to beliefs, it made no reference to locutions or assertions. It instead made reference to *sayings*. Recall the original argument (C):

(C1) If Nihilism and neo-Russellianism are both true, then sometimes competent speakers will sincerely say something that they do not believe.

(C2) Competent speakers never sincerely say something that they do not believe.

(C3) So, Nihilism and neo-Russellianism are not both true.

The Nihilist now has an out: she can claim that only what is asserted is among what is said, and deny (C1). But I believe that this is a mistake. What speakers assert cannot be the only thing that speakers say. In other words, what speakers locute is at least a component of what speakers say. I will remain neutral with regards to whether what speakers assert is also among what is said.

Why should we think that what is locuted must be a component of what is said? Consider a situation in which Jane sincerely utters the sentence "Graham Priest is tall" and does not thereby assert what she locutes. As I just argued, all Invariantists are committed to the possibility of such a circumstance. Suppose, John then reports what Jane said: "Jane said that Graham Priest is tall." This report is clearly accurate. In fact, these kinds of reports are the ones that I (and every other Invariantist) used in order to make the case for Invariantism in the first place. So an Invariantist cannot reject the accuracy of the report without undermining her own position. But, *ex hypothesi*, Jane did not assert that Graham Priest is tall. So it can't be the case that what was said by Jane amounts to what was asserted by Jane. Something more must get into what is said by Jane in order to explain why John's report is accurate. But the best candidate for explaining the accuracy of John's report is that Jane said that Graham Priest is tall by locuting that Graham Priest is tall. As a consequence, we should believe that what is locuted is among what is said.

But if all of these considerations are right, then we have an argument against (C2):

(G1) Invariantism is true.

(G2) If Invariantism is true, sometimes what is locuted is not among what is asserted.

(G3) If sometimes what is locuted is not among what is asserted, then sometimes competent speakers sincerely say something that they do not believe.

(G4) So, sometimes competent speakers sincerely say something that they do not believe.

Since (G4) is a direct denial of (C2), we now have reason to reject (C2) independently of whether Nihilism is the right version of Invariantism.

3.8 Nihilism and Enrichment:

Let us now look at the second argument against neo-Russellian Nihilism. We can imagine a situation where a speaker in a particular contexts utters the sentences

(H1) S: "Graham Priest is tall" (uttered in context *C*)

and

(H2) S: "Graham Priest is smart." (uttered in context *C*)

Unlike the Radicalist and Minimalist, the Nihilist needs to say that both utterances express the same proposition:

(B4) <_______, Graham Priest>

So both the content of (H1) and (H2) and the context of utterance are the same. But it is pretty clear that the two sentences communicate different information. As a result, it is not the case that the context and the content of the sentences together determine what is communicated. This makes communication very mysterious on the Nihilist picture.

I see two ways for the Nihilist to respond to this objection. The first way is to just accept that there are factors beyond content and context that explain what is communicated, and explain why this is not mysterious. The second way is to accept that context and semantic content are all that is needed, but claim that there are some features about the context that mark a relevant difference between "Graham Priest is tall" and "Graham Priest is smart" even when the context of utterance is the same. I'm inclined to go for the second option. As a matter of fact, there are several relevant contextual differences, both conventional and conversational, which can explain why (H1) and (H2) may undergo different enrichment.

One relevant difference between (H1) and (H2), in any context, is that they use different words. This is a fact about the context of utterance, no matter which context these sentences are uttered in. Furthermore, there are conventional implicature rules in place which tell us what words like "tall" and "smart" are used to assert.[60] This should be enough, most of the time, to give us the pragmatically enriched propositions

(H3) <BEING-TALL-IN-SOME-WAY-OR-OTHER, Graham Priest>

(H4) <BEING-SMART-IN-SOME-WAY-OR-OTHER, Graham Priest>

---

[60] See Grice (1975) for further discussion.

which are distinct propositions. (H1) and (H2), as I argued in Chapter 2, are not the semantic content of (H3) and (H4). But this still leaves open the option that (H3) and (H4) are often asserted when (H1) and (H2) are uttered.

This does give us what looks like a problem with the conception of semantics that Soames presents of semantic content as "what all utterances of a sentence have in common". If this is right, then it looks like we might as well call (H3) and (H4) the semantic content of (H1) and (H2). But it is not the case that all utterances of (H1) assert (H3). Consider:

> A and B are absolutists about tallness. They believe that tallness is not relative to anything. As a result, they believe that there is no such thing as BEING-TALL-IN-SOME-WAY-OR-OTHER. They do, however, think that there is such a thing as BEING-TALL. When A and B both look at Graham Priest, A says to B: "Graham Priest is tall".

Did A assert (H3)? Probably not. There is an understanding that A and B do not believe in BEING-TALL-IN-SOME-WAY-OR-OTHER. And A and B are perfectly competent speakers of English. Granted, A and B have strange metaphysical views, but this is not a reason to exclude them from our theory of communication.[61] So A sincerely uttered (H1) without asserting (H3). So (H3) is not what is common among all utterances of (H1). As a result, the pressure to identify (H3) with (H1) disappears.

But if (H3) and (H4) are not the propositions that are asserted by (H1) and (H2) in the context above, which propositions are? This will depend on facts about the conversational background in the context of A and B, but there might be more descriptive propositions such as

(H5) <BEING-AT-LEAST-*N*-CENTIMETRES-IN-HEIGHT, Graham Priest>

(H6) <HAVING-AN-IQ-OF-AT-LEAST-*N*, Graham Priest>

---

[61]One might worry that A and B would have to be irrational in order to be absolutists about tallness. I don't see why this has to be so. Suppose moral relativism is correct. The view that there is a property of BEING-RIGHT while there is no relation of BEING-RIGHT-IN-__-WAY does not seem irrational to me, even under the supposition that it is false. If so, I don't think that the position that A and B are endorsing is irrational either.

The context of utterance and the conversational standards for tallness and smartness will determine exactly which propositions are asserted.

I take it that this picture allows us to explain how different non-denoting predicates can be used in the same context to assert different propositions. As a result, we can now see why (D2) is false. Unlike what it claims, the Nihilist does have an explanation for how context and content together determine what is communicated.

3.9 The Irrelevance of Semantic Content:

There is one final objection to the conjunction of neo-Russelianism and Nihilism. This is an objection raised by Carston (2002) and Recanati (2004) to Minimalism. Recanati says

> What must ultimately be accounted for is what speakers say in the pragmatic sense. The job of characters, contents and so on is to contribute to the overall explanation. But it is sufficient to assign semantic contents (in context) to simple expressions. Pragmatic processes will operate on those contents, and the composition rules will compose the resulting pragmatic values, thereby yielding the content of the speaker's assertion. Of course it is possible to let the composition rules compose the semantic contents of the constituent expressions, thereby yielding the minimal proposition expressed by the sentence. (...). However, the content of the speaker's assertion will still be determined by composing the pragmatic values from the operation of pragmatic processes on the contents of the constituent expressions; so it is unclear what additional job the minimal proposition is supposed to be doing.

Recanati's thought is that, since the locutions of the Invariantist are not among what is asserted, we might as well cut them out of our explanation and hold that the content of a sentence in a context is just what the sentence communicates in that context. After all, what is asserted is the only thing that is really important for communication. And what is asserted seems to be mostly (or maybe completely) determined by the sentence structure and the context. So what reason is there to think that there is semantic content at all? Isn't the idea of an Invariantist proposition explanatorily irrelevant? And if so, shouldn't we just eliminate semantic content altogether, and rest content with speaking of the propositions that are asserted? Put in terms of our considerations regarding Nihilism and neo-Russellianism, we can read the objection as follows:

(E1) If Nihilsm and neo-Russellianism are both true, then semantic content plays no role in explaining communication.

(E2) If semantic content plays no role in explaining communication, then there is no such thing as semantic content.

(E3) If there is no such thing as semantic content, then neo-Russellianism is false.

(E4) So, Nihilism and neo-Russellianism are not both true.

The first thing I want to explain is why I think this is a problem for neo-Russellian Nihilism in a way that it is not a problem for other views. Consider neo-Russellian Minimalism, for example. The picture the Minimalist tells of how what is asserted is determined makes reference to the semantic content of terms in the sentence that is uttered. The Minimalist idea is that this semantic content gets enriched. On a Nihilist picture that is Fregean, this expanation would also work, since terms in uttered sentences would also have semantic contents. But, on a neo-Russellian Nihilist picture, many terms lack semantic content altogether. So, unlike the Minimalist or the Fregean, the neo-Russellian Nihilist has a harder time denying (E1).

I believe, however, that the neo-Russellian Nihilist can deny (E1). This is because the semantic content that is in question here is not the semantic content of terms, but rather the semantic content of sentences. The sentence "Graham Priest is tall" has a *proposition* as its semantic content. As a result, in order for (E1) to be true, it must be the case that all facts about this proposition are irrelevant for determining what is asserted. But the facts about this proposition are not just the facts about the semantic content of its predicates. It also has a subject term, "Graham Priest". Furthermore, it is not just the *constituents* of the proposition that are relevant for determining what is asserted. The *structure* of the proposition is relevant as well. The proposition expressed by "Graham Priest is tall" lacks quantifiers, negations and logical connectives. These are relevant factors for determining what is asserted as well. So the fact that the predicate in "Graham Priest is tall" fails to have any assertion-relevant semantic content does not give us a reason to think that the semantic content of the *sentence* is irrelevant for determining what is asserted.

I would also like to note that (D2) is false as well. We should not think that the explanatory value of semantic content is limited to explaining what is asserted by speakers. As I argued in the previous section, semantic content is necessary for explaining what is *said* by speakers, which cannot reduce to what is *asserted* by them. So, even if it were true that semantic content plays no explanatory role in determining what is asserted, that would still not be a sufficient reason to believe that sentences lack semantic content, or that speakers do not locute any propositions.

3.9 Conclusion

In this chapter, I have dealt with an assortment of objections to Invariantist Nihilism. First, I dismissed the objection that the view is committed to Semantic Nihilism. Even if it is, it is not clear why this is an objection to the view. Then, I discussed some objections that could be raised regarding the conjunction of Nihilism and neo-Russellianism. I replied to objections to the existence of gappy propositions, and objections that attempt to assimilate Nihilism into a kind of Radicalism. I also looked at three objections that claimed that Nihilism and neo-Russellianism make inconsistent claims. The first objection relied on the assumption that what is said sincerely must be believed, which I argued against. The second objection attempted to make communication mysterious on the Nihilist view. I gave an account of communication that I believe can deal with this objection. Finally, the last objection I looked at, argued that semantic content is explanatorily irrelevant, and should be eliminated from our theory of language. I argued that there are reasons to keep semantic content around. Short of any other objections to Nihilism, I take the view to have been given a complete defence.

Works Cited

Adams, Fred, Fuller, Gary, and Stecker, Robert. 2002. "The Semantics of Fictional Names," *Pacific Philosophical Quarterly* 78(2): 128-48.

Bach, Kent. 1997. "Do Belief Reports Report Beliefs?" *Pacific Philosophical Quarterly* 78: 215-241

------ 2006. "The Excluded Middle: Semantic Minimalism without Minimal Propositions," *Philosophy and Phenomenological Research*, 73 (2): 435-442.

------ 2008. "Perspectives on Possibilities: Contextualism, Relativism, or What?" in eds. Egan and Weatherson, *Epistemic Modality*. Oxford University Press.

------ 2012. "Context Dependence," in eds. García-Carpintero and Kölbel *The Continuum Companion to the Philosophy of Language*. Continuum International.

Bealer, George. 1993. "Universals," *Journal of Philosophy*, 60 (1): 5-32.

Braun, David. 1995. "What is Character?" *Journal of Philosophical Logic* 24: 227-240.

------- 2005. "Empty Names, Fictional Names, Mythical Names," *Nous* 39: 596-631.

------- 2006. "Names and Natural Kind Terms," *Handbook of Philosophy of Language*, eds. Lepore and Smith, Oxford University Press.

------- 2012. "An Invariantist Theory of 'Might' Might Be Right," *Linguistics and Philosophy*.

------- 2013. "Contextualism About 'Might' and Says-That Ascriptions," *Philosophical Studies*.

Braun, David, and Sider, Theodore. 2006. "Kripke's Revenge," *Philosophical Studies* 128: 669-82.

------- 2007. "Vague, So Untrue," *Nous* 41: 133-56.

Brandom, Robert. 1994. *Making it Explicit: Reasoning, Representing, and Discursive Commitment*. Harvard University Press.

Buchanan, Ray. 2012. "Is Belief a Propositional Attitude?" *Philosophers' Imprint* 12 (1): 1-20.

Caplan, Ben. "Empty Names." Dissertation at UCLA.

Caplan, Ben, and Tillman, Chris. "Brutal Propositions," manuscript.

Cappelen and Hawthorne. *Relativism and Monadic Truth*

Cappelen, Herman, and Lepore, Ernie. 2002. "Indexicality, Binding, Anaphora, and A Priori Truth," *Analysis 62: 271-81*

------ 2003. "Context Shifting Arguments," *Philosophical Perspectives* 17(1): 25-50

------ 2005. *Insensitive Semantics: A defence of Semantic Minimalism and Speech Act Pluralism.* Blackwell.

-------2006. "Replies" *Philosophy and Phenomenological Research* 73(2): 469-92.

Carston, Robyn. 2002. *Thoughts and Utterances: the Pragmatics of Explicit Communication.* Wiley-Blackwell

Davidson, Donald. 1968. "On Saying That," *Synthese* 19(1-2): 130-146.

DeRose, Keith. 2009. *The Case for Contextualism: Knowledge, Scepticism, and Context.* Oxford University Press.

Evans, Gareth. 1982. *The Varieties of Reference.* Oxford University Press.

Frege, Gottlob. 1892a. "Über Sinn und Bedeutung," *Zeitschrift für Philosophie und Philosophische Kritik* 100: 25-50.

------ 1892b. 'Über Begriff und Gegenstand', *Vierteljahresschrift für wissenschaftliche Philosophie*, 16: 192–205

Grice, H. P. 1975. "Logic and Conversation," in Cole and Morgan (eds.), *Syntax and Semantics 3: Speech Acts.* Academic Press. pp. 41-58.

Hawthorne, John. 2004. *Knowledge and Lotteries.* Oxford University Press.

Kaplan, David. 1989. "Demonstratives," in eds. Almog, Perry, and Wettstein, *Themes from Kaplan.* 481-563.

Keller, Lorraine. Forthcoming. "The Metaphysics of Propositional Constituency," *Canadian Journal of Philosophy*

King, Jeff. 2007. *The Nature and Structure of Content.* Oxford University Press.

Lewis, David. 1986. *On the Plurality of Worlds.* Blackwell Publishing Ltd.

------ 1983. "New Work for a Theory of Universals," *Australasian Journal of Philosophy* 61: 343-77.

McFarlane, John. 2009. "Non-Indexical Contextualism," *Synthese* 166 (2): 231-250.

Moltmann, Friederike. 2003. "Propositional Attitudes without Propositions," *Synthese* 135: 77-118.

Mousavian, Seyed N. 2011. "Gappy Propositions?" *Canadian Journal of Philosophy* 41 (1): 125-157.

Perry, John. "Indexicals, Contexts and Unarticulated Constituents," *Proceedings of the 1995 CLSI-Amsterdam Logic, Language and Computation Conference*. CLSI Publications

Priest, Graham. 2005. *Towards Non-Being: The Logic and Metaphysics of Intentionality*. Oxford University Press.

------- 2006. *In Contradiction: A Study of the Transconsistent.* Oxford University Press

Recanati, François. 2004. *Literal Meaning*. Cambridge University Press.

Russell, Bertrand. 1903. *The Principles of Mathematics*. Cambridge University Press.

Salmon, Nathan. 1986. *Frege's Puzzle*. MIT Press

------- 1998. "Nonexistence," *Nous* 32 (3): 277-319.

Sider, Theodore. 2011. *Writing the Book of the World*. Oxford University Press.

Soames, Scott. 2002. *Beyond Rigidity: The Unfinished Semantic Agenda of Naming and Necessity.* Oxford University Press.

------- 2005. "Naming and Asserting," in Szabo (ed) *Semantics Versus Pragmatics*. Oxford University Press. pp. 356-382.

------- forthcoming. "The Gap Between Meaning and Assertion: Why what we literally say often differs from what our words literally mean," to appear in ed. Hackl and Thornton, *Asserting, Meaning, and Implying*.

Soames, Scott, Speaks, Jeff, and King, Jeff. 2014. *New Thinking About Propositions.* Oxford University Press.

Stalnaker. Robert. 1984. *Inquiry*. MIT Press

Stanley, Jason. 2000. "Context and Logical Form," *Linguistics and Philosophy* 23: 391-434.

Tillman, Chris and Fowler, Gregory. 2012. "Propositions and Parthood: The Universe and Anti-Symmetry. *Australasian Journal of Philosophy* 90 (3): 525-39.

Williamson, Timothy. 1994. *Vagueness*. Routledge.

CPSIA information can be obtained
at www.ICGtesting.com
Printed in the USA
LVHW032015220323
742311LV00014B/1289

9 781805 243786